O9-AHW-674

ASIA

Pacific

20%
40%
60%
80%

80%
60%

AUSTRALIA

40%
20%

8PM   9PM   10PM

Annular
Solar Eclipse

1998
August 21

20%
40%
60%
80%

ASIA

80%
60%
40%
20%

AFRICA

5AM

6AM

7AM

Total
Solar Eclipse

1999
August 11

What do the maps of solar eclipses on the preceding pages show?

North pole

Path of totality

Extent of solar disk obscured

Time of maximum eclipse

Parallel of latitude

Moon's shadow

Path of totality

Border of visibility

Meridian of longitude

How Do I Use the Maps?

The maps on the foldout front flap show total and annular solar eclipses up to the year 2000 and include the exact date and time, as well as how much of the solar disk is obscured.

In a total solar eclipse, the Moon's shadow travels across Earth. The shape of the inner portion of the shadow, the umbra, depends on how it strikes the curved surface of Earth. Because Earth is round, the area covered by the umbra is sometimes elliptical. On both sides of the location of totality (gray band) there is a large area that is reached only by the penumbra. Here the Sun is only partially darkened. The part of the Sun's disk that is covered grows larger the closer one gets to the location of totality. The maps indicate the time (Eastern Standard Time) when the umbra reaches a given point in the location of totality. For places reached by the penumbra, the time when the Sun is most obscured is given. The percentage numbers indicate the maximum obscuring of the solar disk by the Moon. For more on solar eclipses, turn to page 108.

Joachim Ekrutt

Stars and Planets

Identifying Them, Learning about Them, Experiencing Them

With all Important Celestial Events up to the Year 2000
and with a Lexicon of Celestial Bodies

175 Star Maps, Pictures of the Constellations, and Diagrams
30 Color Photos of Celestial Objects

Star Maps and Diagrams by Wil Tirion
Maps of Solar and Lunar Eclipses by Heiner O. Neuendorf

Consulting Editor: Clint Hatchett
Astronomer
Christa McAuliffe Planetarium
Concord, New Hampshire

BARRON'S

Preface/Contents

A clear, starry night, when the sky sparkles and glitters everywhere, arouses our sense of curiosity. What are the names of the stars that shine with such special brilliance? How can one tell the constellations in this confusing multitude of stars? What else is there to see in the sky? There are also spectacular celestial sights, such as solar and lunar eclipses, galaxies, and planets that no devoted stargazer wants to miss. Barron's *Stars and Planets* will keep anybody—whether beginner or experienced hobbyist—abreast of what is going on in the sky through the year 2000. Wil Tirion, an internationally acclaimed astronomical cartographer, has developed especially for this book 72 star maps that will help anybody get oriented in the sky at first try. The maps always show the section of the sky that one actually sees when looking north or south. Marked in these monthly maps are all the stars and constellations that are clearly distinguishable to the naked eye. And the maps can be used worldwide!

A special and novel feature in this book is its maps of the globe printed in color. They show at a glance when and where solar and lunar eclipses will be visible during the entire decade of the 1990s. This is a feature that amateur astronomers (who do not want to miss these thrilling events) will appreciate. But that is not all: In an astronomical calendar all the most beautiful heavenly events—such as planets in easily viewable positions—are listed in easy-to-consult tables. The book also contains many helpful illustrations, accompanied by precise explanations, as well as a chapter on basic astronomy for beginners and a "Lexicon of Celestial Bodies," which serves as a useful reference and at the same time makes fascinating reading in its own right. All in all, this handbook of the decade is both a tool to help you identify what you see in the sky and a descriptive account that brings the heavens closer.

The author and editors of *Stars and Planets* wish you many happy and exciting hours of stargazing.

8 Astronomy Made Easy

8 The Movement of Earth
8 How the Celestial Spheres and Earth Are Alike
9 North Pole, South Pole, and Equator
10 Fixed Stars Are Not as Immobile as They Seem
11 The Origin of the Constellations
11 The Sun—The Star of Our Solar System
12 Dusk, Midnight Sun, and Polar Night
13 What Causes the Seasons of the Year?
13 What Time Is It Where?
15 Everything about the Apparent Path of the Sun
15 The Constellations and the Zodiac
16 The Moon and the Planets

19 Identifying and Experiencing the Stars

19 What Do the Star Maps Include?
19 Which Star Map Applies Where?
20 The Constellations and Their History
21 Symbols Used in the Star Maps
22 Which Stars Do You Look for First?
23 Practical Tips on Identifying Stars
24 Watching the Sky through Binoculars

27 Star Map Series N I

53 Star Map Series N II

79 Star Map Series S

104 Celestial Events up to the Year 2000

104 Predictable Facts Concerning the Sun, Earth, and the Beginning of the Seasons
105 All Phases of the Moon Can Be Predicted Accurately
108 Dates, Duration, and Visibility of Solar Eclipses
112 Dates, Duration, and Visibility of Lunar Eclipses

4

Contents

The Lagoon Nebula in Sagittarius, a glowing cloud of hydrogen gas (see page 142).

116   Mars, the Red Planet
116   Jupiter in a Yellowish Light
116   Saturn, the Planet in White

119   **Astronomical Calendar 1992–2000**

130   **Lexicon of Celestial Bodies**

154   **Index**

158   **Planetaria and Observatories**

Photo on following two pages: Saturn and its ▷ moons: a spectacular photo montage of pictures taken by the space probe Voyager I.

113   The Planets Appear in the Constellations of the Zodiac
114   Mercury Appears Only Briefly
115   Venus, the Morning and Evening Star

Star map N I/1, January, north.

*The photos on the cover show:
Front cover: The star cluster of the Pleiades; the planet Saturn; a partial solar eclipse.
Back cover: Star map N I/1, January, south; Perseus from star map NI/2 north and Capricornus from star map S 11 south. These illustrations are from Hevelius's sky atlas.
Spine of book: Lunar eclipse.*

WEST   NORTH   EAST

Astronomy Made Easy

A stronomy is one of the oldest sciences. Human beings have gazed up at the starry skies from time immemorial, and they recognized early on that strict laws govern the movement of the stars. The most important results of thousands of years of observation help us even today in studying and understanding the night skies.

The Movement of Earth

Our planet Earth is an almost perfect sphere with a diameter of 7,918 miles (12,756 km). It revolves around its own axis—an imaginary line that runs from the north pole to the south pole—with great precision. This rotation happens at an extremely fast rate. Thus, any point along the equator circles around the center of Earth at a speed of 1,036 miles (1,669 km) per hour. We are, however, completely unaware of this motion because everything rotates along with us—the air, the land, the oceans, our entire natural environment.

Earth takes 24 hours to revolve once. This is the basis of our measurement of time. Earth rotates from west to east. It would be extremely hard to prove that this motion actually takes place if it were not for the stars way beyond Earth's atmosphere. Unlike the surface of Earth, they remain still all day and all night. But because of Earth's revolving motion, they seem to travel across the sky in the opposite direction from Earth's rotation, namely from east to west. It follows that the rising in the east of stars, the Moon, the Sun, and all other heavenly bodies and their setting in the west are only illusions of movement produced by the rotation of Earth in the opposite direction.

Only very late, in the nineteenth century, were methods found that could prove without reliance on observation of the stars that Earth does indeed rotate around its axis. Probably the most famous of these methods is Foucault's pendulum, which is based on a brilliant experiment thought up by the French physicist Jean Bernard Léon Foucault. In 1851, Foucault had a pendulum hung in the dome of the famous Paris Pantheon. Because Earth rotates, the floor beneath the pendulum clearly shifted while the pendulum, on account of inertia, remained stationary. This was a sensational experiment that convincingly demonstrated to the fascinated public of the last century that Earth actually rotates and that it is not the stars that race around us at dizzying speeds, as people had so long imagined from ancient days through the Middle Ages.

How the Celestial Spheres and Earth Are Alike

Although we know today that there is no such thing as a celestial sphere—let alone one fashioned of crystal—from which the stars are somehow hung, this old way of picturing the world still has its uses. Let us imagine Earth, the terrestrial sphere, as a balloon that can be inflated until it touches this imaginary celestial sphere. If the surface of the inflated balloon Earth were marked with stamp ink, the most important lines on it would be transferred to the celestial sphere. Earth's equator (see diagram, page 9) would translate into the celestial equator, and the same would happen with the lines indicating longitude and latitude. The north geographic pole would mark the north celestial pole and the south geographic pole would yield the south celestial pole. This is exactly how astronomers look at the sky even today. The celestial equator divides the celestial sphere into a northern and a southern half, and the north and south celestial poles indicate the points in the celestial sphere that do not move along with the rotation but mark the axis around which the rotation takes place. Almost directly over the north celestial pole stands the famous North Star (see diagram, page 22). The south celestial pole is not marked by any particularly noticeable star (see page 22).

With the aid of this (imaginary) celestial sphere and the terrestrial sphere, it is easy to explain and picture the various movements of the heavenly bodies.

North Pole, South Pole, and Equator

An observer standing on Earth's north or south pole would find the celestial north or south pole directly overhead because Earth's axis is identical with that of the celestial sphere. For this observer, the pole is at the highest point of the visible sky, the zenith (see diagram below), and seen from here, all stars move along a path parallel to the horizon, which is the limit of the visible half of the heavens. The equator of the celestial sphere coincides exactly with the horizon. Hence only half the sky is visible throughout the entire year. Scientists at the Ameri-

can Scott-Amundsen south polar research station consequently see the same stars revolve continuously around them during the southern winter months.

The other extreme exists at the equator. Here the celestial equator rises up in an imaginary vertical line from the horizon and runs through the zenith, the highest point of the sky. The north celestial pole lies exactly on the horizon, as does the south celestial pole. An observer here can see all the stars of the sky. The stars in the east rise straight up in the east and sink straight down again below the horizon in the west.

For all geographical latitudes lying between these two extremes, there is a part of the sky that always remains invisible. It is the part surrounding the celestial pole of the opposite hemisphere. Thus, on Earth's

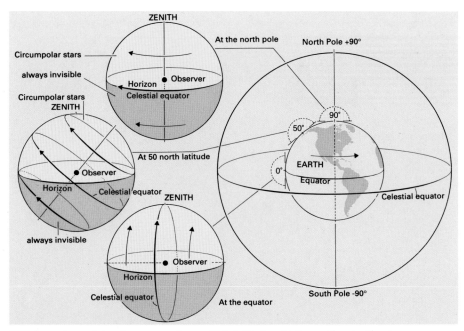

Which portions of the sky are seen from which latitudes: At the north pole, the stars move parallel to the horizon; at the equator, they move up and down vertically; in between (at about 50° north) they move at a diagonal.

Northern Hemisphere the area around the south celestial pole remains hidden. On the other hand, the area of the sky that is close to the visible pole remains in view all the time. It never "sets" but seems to circle around the celestial pole. The photo on page 129 shows this in a very striking fashion. These stars, which never set, are called circumpolar stars because they seem to revolve continually around the pole. The closer one is to the pole, the more circumpolar stars there are. This is because at the poles an entire celestial hemisphere seems to rotate parallel to the horizon and all the visible stars become circumpolar.

Note: For identifying the stars, only the latitude of the observation point matters.

Consequently a stargazer in Canada sees the same stars as someone watching the skies in central Europe or in northern Japan.

Similarly, Buenos Aires, Cape Town, and Adelaide (Australia) all see the same star patterns overhead; in all three places the same stars are circumpolar and the same stars are invisible because they remain below the horizon all the time.

Fixed Stars Are Not as Immobile as They Seem

The earliest people who watched the starry skies several thousand years ago noticed that the stars rise and set but that apart from this motion they remain—with some remarkable exceptions—stationary in relation to one another. Sirius, for example, the brightest of all the stars, is always the same distance away from, say, Aldebaran or the twin stars Castor and Pollux. For this reason these stars were very early called "fixed" stars, that is, stars that seem to have their firm, fixed, and immovable place in the firmament. This was before people realized

A photo taken with long time exposure shows the stars as tracks of light created by Earth's rotation.

The Constellations

that it is Earth's spinning around its own axis that causes the apparent rising and setting of the stars. In those times people believed that all the celestial bodies were located on a large, crystal orb that revolved around Earth at dizzying speeds. Today we know, of course, that the stars are not immovable objects attached to a heavenly vault.

The Origin of the Constellations

The so-called fixed stars are such inconceivably large distances away from Earth that their motion would lead to a perceptible change of the star patterns only over an extremely long time span, perhaps over tens of thousands of years. The distances between stars are therefore measured not in miles but in light-years. One light-year, the distance traveled by a light ray in one year (at a speed of 186,000 miles or 300,000 km per second), is equal to 5.88 trillion miles (9.46 trillion km) that is, rounded off, a 6 followed by 12 zeroes. Even our very closest stellar neighbor, Alpha Centauri (see pages 130–31), is 4.3 light-years distant, and most other stars are considerably farther away. Viewed from such a literally astronomical remove, even the immense distances traveled by the stars shrink to angles too small to be measured. So today we still see the stars in practically the identical places where they appeared to the ancient Egyptians and Babylonians 4,000 to 5,000 years ago.

Given the apparent permanence of the stars' locations relative to each other, only a small step was required to arrive at the idea of constellations. Many of the earliest civilizations thought they recognized certain shapes in the patterns made up by the apparently immobile stars, and they imaginatively identified these shapes with figures from their myths and legends. This is how the constellations came into being, and they have become one of the most important symbols of the starry heavens. They are also of considerable help in getting oriented in the night sky, and they are still of great significance even in modern astronomy. What constellations are visible, where they are in relation to each other, and the stories behind their names are subjects covered in the texts accompanying the star maps for each month (starting on page 27).

The Sun—The Star of Our Solar System

There is one star whose rising and setting is of supreme importance to us, namely, the Sun. Because of Earth's rotation, the Sun, like the other stars, rises in the east, travels across the sky, and sets in the west. In the Southern Hemisphere, too—in Cape Town or in Melbourne, for instance—the Sun rises in the eastern sky. It reaches its zenith in the north, and then sinks below the horizon in the west. This rising and setting of the Sun is what gives us our bright days and dark nights and thus the most basic divisions of time determining our daily lives.

When the Sun rises above the horizon all the other stars near it fade because of the sun's intense brightness. Earth's atmosphere contributes significantly to the dominance of the Sun's light because it diffuses the Sun's rays so much across the entire visible celestial hemisphere that the light of no other heavenly bodies can compete with it—with the exception of the Moon and occasionally the planet Venus. Because of their considerable brightness, Venus and the Moon sometimes can be seen even during daylight. The stars, however, don't become visible until the Sun has disappeared below the western horizon.

There is no abrupt transition from brightness of day to darkness of night. Day and night are separated by a period of dusk, during which the sky gradually darkens in the east while sunlight still glows above the horizon for some time in the west. The stars don't appear until later, well after the Sun has set. Dusk, too, is caused by Earth's atmosphere, which continues to diffuse sunlight across the sky even after the Sun has sunk below the horizon.

Dusk, Midnight Sun, and Polar Night

Astronomers distinguish between different phases of dusk, phases that are always dependent on geographic latitude. This is because the Sun, like the stars, sets at varying angles to the horizon (see diagram below). At the equator and in the tropics in general—that is, at low geographic latitudes—dusk is very brief because the Sun travels toward the horizon along a vertical path and therefore drops deep below it very quickly. In the mid-latitudes dusk lasts considerably longer, and in the extreme north-

ern and southern latitudes, finally, we enter regions where the Sun at certain periods of the year no longer descends low enough to allow for real darkness. These are the times of the famous white nights and the midnight sun, when the Sun no longer sets but becomes "circumpolar" itself. It never sets during the 24 hours of the day, that is, during Earth's entire daily rotation. Observers anywhere within one of the polar circles, which are located at 66.5 degrees north latitude and 66.5 degrees south latitude, respectively—places like Tromsö and Murmansk, for example—experience this unique phenomenon. For several weeks and even months the Sun never sets, and six months later it fails to rise for a similar period,

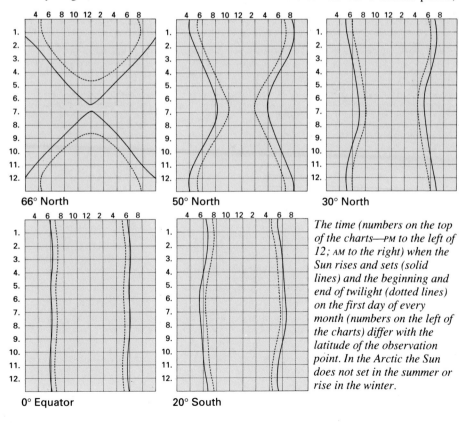

66° North   50° North   30° North

0° Equator   20° South

The time (numbers on the top of the charts—PM to the left of 12; AM to the right) when the Sun rises and sets (solid lines) and the beginning and end of twilight (dotted lines) on the first day of every month (numbers on the left of the charts) differ with the latitude of the observation point. In the Arctic the Sun does not set in the summer or rise in the winter.

creating the so-called polar night. The most extreme conditions are again found at the actual north and south poles, where the Sun is above the horizon for slightly over six months and remains below it for slightly less than six months.

All these phenomena—varying length of day, midnight sun, the polar night, as well as the seasons of the year—are the result of two facts: the movement of Earth around the Sun and the angle of Earth's axis in space (see diagram below).

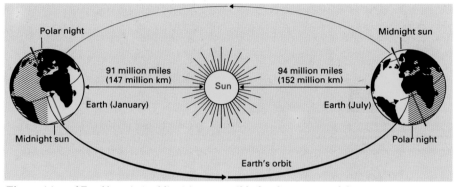

The position of Earth's axis (red line) is responsible for the seasons of the year.

What Causes the Seasons of the Year?

Earth not only revolves around its own axis but also moves around the Sun. The time Earth takes to complete one journey around the Sun (at an average velocity of about 18 miles or 30 km per second) is one year, which is the second time unit on which our measuring of time is based. To be exact, Earth takes 365 days, 5 hours, 48 minutes, and 46 seconds for one complete revolution around the Sun. In other words, Earth has rotated around its own axis 365¼ times by the time it has completed one circuit around the Sun. However, Earth's axis of rotation is not perpendicular to the plane of its orbit around the Sun but is instead at an angle of precisely 66½ degrees. This fact has significant consequences. Our seasons and all the phenomena described above are the result of this tilt of Earth's axis away from the perpendicular to its orbiting plane.

The above diagram illustrates the situation: At one time (in mid-December) Earth turns its southern half toward the Sun while

the northern half faces away from the Sun. At this point the Sun is very high in the sky in the Southern Hemisphere and describes a large arc that leaves it shining much longer than 12 hours.

On the Northern Hemisphere, things are just the opposite: The Sun's rays emanate from low in the sky; they no longer reach the polar region, where the polar night reigns. In the Southern Hemisphere it is summer; in the Northern Hemisphere, winter.

Six months later (in mid-June), conditions are reversed. In between (in spring and autumn) the Sun shines down straight on the equator. For a short while, conditions are the same everywhere on Earth: The Sun shines for 12 hours everywhere, and the night also lasts 12 hours (on the seasons, see also page 104).

What Time Is It Where?

The rising and setting of the Sun also determines the time our clocks indicate. Our clocks imitate the heavenly clock, where the

13

Sun functions as a hand that indicates the time. We say it's 12 noon when the Sun reaches its highest point in the south (or, in the Southern Hemisphere, the north), and it's midnight when the Sun has sunk to its lowest point, invisible below the horizon. This model is much simplified. Our clocks indicate the time of day it is at a given meridian of longitude, and their rhythm is fine-tuned in accordance with an atomic clock. But even our modern time, which is defined by atomic clocks, still needs adjustment at irregular intervals to conform to the exact position of Earth in relation to the Sun.

All the times given in this book are in Eastern Standard Time (EST). EST corresponds exactly to the Sun's time on the 75th meridian of longitude west of Greenwich. To specify a location on the geographic globe, two coordinates are used: longitude and latitude. Latitude measures the distance from the equator both north and south. It is expressed in degrees or parallels of latitude, which, as the latter name suggests, run parallel to the equator. Longitude is the north-south coordinate. It also is measured in degrees, in this case counted east and west

starting from the zero or prime meridian, which is the meridian that runs through the Royal Observatory in Greenwich, England. For purposes of practicality, the globe has been divided into time zones an average of 75 degrees wide, within which the same time, the so-called zone time, holds. The time difference from one zone to the next is one hour.

In addition to Eastern Standard Time, there are many other time zones, the most important of which is Greenwich Mean Time (GMT) and Universal Time because many astronomical events are referred to in this time. Today Great Britain and Portugal are among the countries that go by GMT. Spain, France, Germany, and Italy, among other countries, use Central European Time (CET). East of the CET zone one shifts to East European Time, which is in force in Romania, Greece, and Turkey among other countries. With the aid of the world time zone map below it is easy to translate EST or GMT into other local times. For places east of Europe, add the number of zones between 0 (Greenwich) and your zone to the local time; for places west of Europe, subtract the

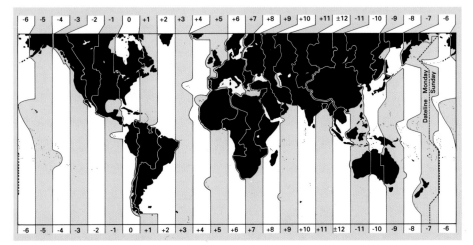

The difference in time from one geographical time zone to the next is one hour.

number. Thus, for example, the beginning of spring for the year 2000 is given on page 104 as March 20 at 2:35 A.M. For someone living in Germany this would mean that spring starts at 8:35 A.M. local time, whereas the clocks in Tokyo would say 16:35 or 4:35 P.M.

Many countries observe daylight saving time during the summer. This is done to save energy, as the name implies. For half the year (in the United States it is always from the first Sunday in April to the last Sunday in October) the clocks are set one hour ahead of standard time, that is, they indicate the Sun's time of the zone one slot to the east. All the heavenly bodies then rise one hour later according to the clock, and the Sun shines less brightly on the still sleeping cities in the morning and sets one hour later. Evening, thus artificially postponed, lasts one hour longer. When daylight saving time is in effect, all indicated times have to have one hour added to them. This turns EST into EDT (Eastern Daylight Saving Time). When using the world time zone map, one has to be careful because other countries also institute daylight saving time, but its period may not coincide exactly with that of EDT. Only if the United States and the country you are interested in have daylight saving time for the same period can you use a given star map without adaptation. Otherwise there will be a difference of minus one hour (for places east) or plus one hour (for places west).

Note: If you want to find out where and for how long daylight saving time is in effect and what time zone applies to a given place, the flight schedules of air lines offer exact information.

Everything about the Apparent Path of the Sun

Just as for a long time—until experiments such as Foucault's pendulum were invented—Earth's rotation could only be deduced indirectly from the apparent move-

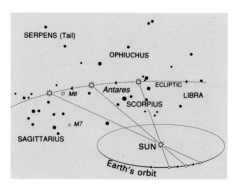

Because of Earth's movement, the Sun seems to travel from star to star.

ment of the firmament, the rising and descending of the stars, so Earth's movement through space could be recognized only indirectly by studying the movement of the Sun or, more accurately, its apparent movement. The Sun is much closer to Earth than the fixed stars. The latter are many hundred thousand times farther away from us. A glance at the diagram at the top of the page shows that from different points on Earth's orbit we see the Sun standing *in front of* different stars in the sky. The Sun seems to move and appears sometimes in front of more northerly constellations and at other times in front of more southerly ones. This apparent circular path the Sun takes across the sky in the course of a year is called the *ecliptic*. The Sun takes exactly one year for its journey around the entire celestial sphere, the same time Earth takes to orbit around the Sun. The Sun's apparent movement across the sky in front of the stars always follows the same path, the ecliptic. This word, which is derived from the Greek word *ekleipsis*, which means to omit or fail, is obviously related to *eclipse*. The imaginary path of the Sun is named the ecliptic because the Sun and Moon are always on the line of the ecliptic during solar and lunar eclipses (see pages 108 and 112). Astronomers of ancient Babylon already recognized this fact several

15

thousand years before Christ. The ecliptic is one of the most important lines in the sky, and it is drawn into all the star maps as a broken line.

The Constellations and the Zodiac

Twelve or, to be more precise, 13 constellations lie along the ecliptic, and the Sun appears to pass through only these constellations in the course of a year. They are the famous constellations of the zodiac, which are among the very oldest constellations. They are:

The Constellations of the Zodiac	
Aries the Ram (April 18)	Scorpius the Scorpion (November 22)
Taurus the Bull (May 13)	Ophiuchus the Serpent Bearer (November 29)
Gemini the Twins (June 21)	Sagittarius the Archer (December 18)
Cancer the Crab (July 20)	Capricornus the Goat (January 19)
Leo the Lion (August 10)	Aquarius the Water Bearer (February 16)
Virgo the Virgin (September 16)	Pisces the Fishes (March 11)
Libra the Balance (October 30)	

The dates in parentheses indicate the days on which the Sun enters the various constellations.

These dates bear no relation to those that are used in horoscopes.

The name zodiac is not altogether accurate because the constellations do not all represent animals but also include some human figures (Gemini, Virgo, Sagittarius, and Aquarius) as well as an object (Libra). Ophiuchus the Serpent Bearer is a completely different case. It did not figure in the classical zodiac at all. It is only since 1930, when the boundaries of all the constellations were revised, that Ophiuchus, which extends into the ecliptic belt next to Scorpius, has been counted among the zodiacal constellations (see pages 66–67).

All stars in the immediate vicinity of the bright Sun are invisible to us because they traverse the daytime sky along with the Sun. It is the stars on the opposite side of the heavens at any given time that we see in the night sky. When the Sun, on its apparent journey across the sky, reaches these stars half a year later, then those we saw earlier become invisible. Now the stars we couldn't see earlier lie opposite the Sun and can be seen at night. Thus the Sun determines which part of the starry sky we see at different times of the year.

The Moon and the Planets

The apparent path of the Sun, the ecliptic, is of great importance in orienting oneself in the night sky. For the Moon and the planets move along the same line, that is, they are always seen only within the 13 zodiacal constellations. Thus all the conspicuous celestial bodies move near the ecliptic.

Apart from the Sun, the Moon is the most prominent object in the sky. Except for the Sun, it is the only celestial object in which we can distinguish surface details with the unaided eye. There are lighter and darker spots that taken together and with a little bit of imagination can be seen as the famous "man in the moon" (for more on the Moon as a celestial body, see page 141). The Moon passes by the stars of the zodiac once every month and is never more than 5 degrees north or south of the ecliptic. During its orbit it goes through its famous phases, appearing in the sky now as half-moon, now as full moon, and, at new moon, disappearing from view altogether. Several times a year it causes the most striking celestial events of all, solar and lunar eclipses. Eclipses and the phases of the Moon are among the most dramatic variable events that take place in the sky, and they therefore are described in detail starting on page 105.

Planets are heavenly bodies that revolve around the Sun like Earth. Our Sun has nine planets that are up to 3.7 billion miles (6 billion km) away from it and orbit around it at various speeds. Together with innumerable smaller bodies—the comets (see page 133), meteorites (see page 138), and minor planets (see page 143)—they make up the solar system. All the bodies of the solar system are lit up by the Sun's light, and it is this light that they reflect toward Earth. In contrast to this, the fixed stars and all other heavenly bodies, such as galaxies, nebulas, and star clusters (see pages 135, 141, and 147), generate their own light.

The planets' order from the Sun is easy to remember with the aid of this mnemonic sentence in which the first letters of the words are the initials of planets' names: **My Very Eagle-eyed Mother Just Spotted Umpteen New Planets.**

Five planets can be seen without the aid of a telescope or binoculars. They are the most luminous celestial bodies after the Sun and the Moon and almost always outshine even the brightest stars. The planets move along the ecliptic from one zodiacal constellation to the next. This moving or "wandering" results from the planets' revolving around the Sun, a fact reflected in the word planet, which is derived from the Greek word *planasthai*, to wander. The precise positions of the planets during the coming years are described starting on page 113.

The nine major planets, as well as Halley's Comet, orbit around the Sun.
The planets Saturn, Jupiter, and Mars as seen from Earth through a telescope.

17

Identifying and Experiencing the Stars

Y ou need some theoretical background plus a bit of practical know-how to find your way around the night sky. But it is really quite amazing how little is required to get one's bearings in the vastness of the starry heavens. Start out by learning everything necessary for using the star maps that follow.

What Do the Star Maps Include?

The maps starting on page 27 include all the stars down to what is called the fourth magnitude, that is, all the stars easily visible to the naked eye. Fainter stars that barely can be discerned without magnification actually are visible these days only far away from cities and other lights and only under the best atmospheric conditions. The size of the yellow dot marking a star shows the star's brightness. The larger the dot, the brighter the star. The ten brightest stars—those that remain visible even against the artificially illuminated night sky of big cities—are indicated by small rays emanating from the dots. They are discussed separately in the lexicon section at the end of the book starting on page 130.

The solid lines linking groups of stars together indicate the constellations. Today 88 constellations, with boundaries defined by a commission of the International Astronomical Union in 1930, are recognized. They extend across the entire sky leaving no areas unaccounted for. Some of these constellations are made up of stars fainter than the fourth magnitude, and they therefore are not mentioned in this book. The star maps depict 62 constellations, all of which are clearly visible. The lines connecting groups of stars indicate especially striking configurations that formed the basis of the stories associated with the constellations and are thus directly responsible for their names. Every view of the sky is described in detail in the text below the maps.

◁ *The Big Dipper shining over the Calar Alto observatory in Spain.*

Which Star Map Applies Where?

The star maps are organized in three series, one each for three latitudinal zones, namely:

- 40 to 60 degrees north (NI)
- 20 to 40 degrees north (NII)
- 10 to 30 degrees south (S)

The first thing to do, therefore, is to determine in which of these zones your observation point is located. The geographic map preceding each series helps you do this.

The next step is to figure out the time when you wish to observe the sky. All the star maps reflect the sky as it appears at exactly the beginning of the month at 11 P.M., the middle of the month at 10 P.M., and the end of the month at 9 P.M.

If daylight saving time is in effect in a given location, an hour has to be added to these times, making them midnight for the beginning, 11 P.M. for the middle, and 10 P.M. for the end of the month.

No adjustments need to be made for the different time zones shown in the map on page 14. The times given are local times that apply to all the zones. Whether you watch the sky in San Francisco at 11 P.M. Pacific Standard Time, or at 11 P.M. Central European Time in Austria, the same chart applies. In some time zones the time difference between the western and eastern boundaries is more than one hour, but this inaccuracy is of no practical significance given the small scale of the maps. Only daylight saving time has to be taken into account because it throws the validity of all of the maps off by one hour. But there is a note to this effect on the maps where this may be the case.

If you want to watch the stars at some other hour, you will have to refer to the table on page 20. First find the month at the top, then the desired time of night at the left. Where the column from the top and the line from the left intersect there is a number that indicates the star map to be used.

Here are two examples:

Let's say you would like to watch the stars in Italy (the world map shows that you have to use the series NII) at 1 A.M. on July 20. In July it is daylight saving time, which means that you have to subtract one hour from what your watch says, that is, you have to find the line indicating midnight. At the intersection of the column for mid-July and the horizontal bar for 11 to 12 P.M. you find the number 8. Consequently you should turn to chart NII/8 on page 68.

Or: You are in South Africa and want to know if the Southern Cross is visible on December 28 at 3:30 A.M. December 28 can be considered the beginning of January, and where the two appropriate lines intersect you find—nothing! The missing part of the sky lies between what is shown on maps 3 and 4. Turn to map S3 (South Africa!) on page 85 and, if the star you are looking for is close to the horizon, also consult S4 on page 87.

Don't worry about the fact that you are using maps labeled August (in the first example) and March (in the second) even though you are observing in July and December, respectively. The months given apply only for the usual stargazing time from 9 to 11 P.M. (or 10 to 12 P.M. daylight saving time).

How Do I Find the Right Star Map?

	Jan. B. M.	Feb. B. M.	Mar. B. M.	April B. M.	May B. M.	June B. M.	July B. M.	Aug. B. M.	Sept. B. M.	Oct. B. M.	Nov. B. M.	Dec. B. M.
6–7 PM	11	12	1	2	3	4	5	6	7	8	9	10
7–8 PM	12	1	2	3	4	5	6	7	8	9	10	11
8–9 PM	12	1	2	3	4	5	6	7	8	9	10	11
9–10 PM	1	2	3	4	5	6	7	8	9	10	11	12
10–11 PM	1	2	3	4	5	6	7	8	9	10	11	12
11–12 PM	2	3	4	5	6	7	8	9	10	11	12	1
12–1 AM	2	3	4	5	6	7	8	9	10	11	12	1
1–2 AM	3	4	5	6	7	8	9	10	11	12	1	2
2–3 AM	3	4	5	6	7	8	9	10	11	12	1	2
3–4 AM	4	5	6	7	8	9	10	11	12	1	2	3
4–5 AM	4	5	6	7	8	9	10	11	12	1	2	3
5–6 AM	5	6	7	8	9	10	11	12	1	2	3	4

Important note: B = Beginning of month; M = Middle of month. Numerals in the columns under B and M designate the month of the correct map: 1 = January, 2 = February, 3 = March, etc. When daylight saving time is in effect (normally from April to October), one hour has to be added to the times given in the table. Perhaps a simpler method is to subtract one hour from the time, according to your watch, when you plan to observe the stars and use this time when consulting the above table.

The Constellations and Their History

To illustrate some of the old myths associated with the constellations, details from a famous sky atlas created by the Danzig astronomer Johannes Hevelius (1611–1687) have been reproduced. In this atlas, figures from Greek mythology are depicted as well as ones of more recent origin. Only in a few cases can one readily see how a star pattern inspired the name of its constellation. If you compare the figures from the Hevelius atlas with the stars in the sky, you will notice that the former show a mirror image of what we see overhead. Hevelius depicted the heavenly sphere as seen from the outside, so to speak.

What the Symbols in the Star Maps Mean

Especially bright stars have proper names of their own. The names of stars like Sirius, Capella, and Aldebaran have been passed down from generation to generation and are, like the figures of the constellations, of ancient origin. Whereas most of today's constellations go back to Greek mythology, the stars were named by Arabian astronomers in the period between A.D. 600 and 1000.

Fainter stars are designated according to a system devised by Johann Bayer (1572–1625), a German lawyer and astronomer who published a famous sky atlas, the *Uranometria*, in 1603 in Augsburg. In this atlas he not only introduced many new constellations that are still recognized today but also invented a very practical system for naming stars, based on the Greek alphabet. The brightest star is named alpha (α), the second brightest, beta (β), and so on. Added to the Greek letter is the genitive of the constellation's Latin name.

Star Designations in the Star Maps

α Cen = Alpha in Centaurus
δ Cep = Delta in Cepheus
ε Lyr = Epsilon in Lyra
ε Aur = Epsilon in Auriga
η Car = Eta in Carina
χ Per = Chi in Perseus
ω Cen = Omega in Centaurus

Later on, astronomers also used regular Latin letters, as, for example, in h Per (= h in Perseus) or L₂ Pup (= L_2 in Puppis).

Symbols Used in the Star Maps

The star maps also show other celestial objects, which are represented by the following symbols:

◆ **Multiple stars:** Here two or more stars revolve around each other in space, but to the unaided eye they appear as two stars that are exceptionally close to each other (see Binaries, page 131).

◉ **Variable stars:** In contrast to most other stars, the brightness of variable stars fluctuates (see pages 150–51).

□ **Nebulas:** Between the stars there are immense gas and dust clouds, some of which appear in the most amazing colors and shapes and count among the most beautiful objects of the night sky (see pages 141–42).

⁖ **Star clusters:** The stars are not distributed evenly across the sky but often are concentrated in certain spots. Such aggregations of stars are called clusters. Astronomers distinguish between open and globular star clusters (see page 147).

○ **Galaxies:** Galaxies are large star systems distributed throughout the universe. The distances that separate them from Earth—millions of light-years—are so immense that our imagination fails to grasp them (see page 135).

Nebulas, star clusters, and galaxies are indicated on the star maps by the letter M followed by a number; for instance, M 31 or M 8. M stands for Charles Messier, a French astronomer (1730–1817) who in 1771 published a catalog of celestial objects that appear cloudlike through a telescope. His catalog designations still are in use today.

All these objects are described in the text below the relevant star maps (pages 27 and following) and/or in the lexicon section starting on page 130.

Finally, the charts also show the night sky's most unusual feature, the luminous band of the Milky Way, which is depicted in the maps as a whitish area. The Milky Way is made up of the combined light of many millions of stars that are not individually visible but whose collective brightness is clearly apparent. The Milky Way snakes across the entire starry sky and in some places breaks up into branches. Its course and some especially interesting aspects of it

21

are described in the text accompanying the appropriate maps and, under its own heading, on page 140.

Which Stars Do You Look for First?

Once you have determined which map to consult, you have to get oriented, that is, you have to figure out approximately where geographical north and south are. Here are a few pointers: In the Northern Hemisphere, Polaris, or the North Star, is a safe guidepost because for all practical purposes it is identical with the north celestial pole. If you draw a vertical line down from it with your eyes to the horizon, you are facing north. The North Star—and consequently the north celestial pole—is located most easily by first finding the best known star pattern, the Big Dipper (part of the constellation Ursa Major), which is circumpolar down to almost the middle of the geographic zone N II and

therefore never disappears below the horizon in those northern latitudes.

Note: If the imaginary line connecting the two stars that form the ladle's edge away from the handle is extended, it leads directly to the north celestial pole. This way you will know where north is (see drawing below, left).

In the Southern Hemisphere, the Southern Cross will help you get oriented relatively easily. If the central axis of the Cross is extended, it points more or less accurately to the south celestial pole. Directly underneath the pole is geographic south (see drawing below, right).

Once you have established the directions in the sky, you are ready for further exploration. By comparing the map with the sky, you will find it relatively easy to locate individual constellations and stars. It is best to

The two stars at the front of the bowl of the dipper point at the north celestial pole.

The central axis of the Southern Cross points at the south celestial pole.

use a dimmed flashlight for reading the maps. If possible, you should do your stargazing when the horizon is dark and there is little interference from artificial light. This is, of course, practically impossible in today's cities, where the sky is usually so bright that one can make out only the most brilliant stars.

Because of this, the very brightest stars— those that are visible even in the lit up skies above big cities—are marked in the maps with little rays. Start out by finding these stars first. Then see if you can find less radiant stars, which are indicated in the charts by smaller dots.

When exploring the sky, it is best to look for constellations. The thin connecting lines in the maps show the approximate outlines of the constellations as they actually are seen in the sky. Start with the brightest visible star and try to memorize the pattern formed by the nearby stars. If this pattern conforms to the picture in the map, you can go on and identify fainter stars and constellations. Without the help of the prominent constellation patterns, it would be a lot harder finding one's way around in the sky.

Below each sky map the most noticeable stars and constellations are described. Also noted are exceptional celestial events of the past. However, the brightest objects in the sky, the planets, do not appear in the maps at all because they move too fast. Therefore, if you spot an especially bright point of light in the sky that you cannot find in the map, check first to see if it is in the ecliptic. If it is—that is, if it appears in the constellations of the zodiac—you can turn to pages 113 and following to check which planets are visible in a particular year and month.

Practical Tips on Identifying Stars

It is always hard to get oriented in the sky when there are only a few stars out. If that is the case, it is better to wait a while, until you begin to recognize some of the constellations, that is, until the positions of indi-

vidual stars in relation to each other become apparent.

In the north, Ursa Major, the Great Bear, with its well-known Big Dipper (called the Plough in England), is of great help in getting started. Once you have identified it, you know where north is and then it is easy to find other constellations (see drawing on page 22).

When dusk has just fallen and the western sky is still lit up by the setting Sun, all you can see are the brightest planets. A brilliant dot in the western sky is then almost always Venus, the evening star. When dawn begins to brighten the sky shortly before sunrise, what you see is usually again Venus, now figuring as the morning star (see page 151).

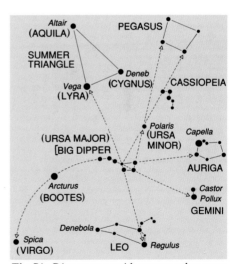

The Big Dipper as a guide post to other stars.

Note: The light of the planets does not flicker but is almost always steady. The stars, by contrast, often flicker or twinkle very noticeably, especially near the horizon. This is caused by turbulences in Earth's atmosphere. The steady light of the planets is one

23

A dust cloud in the constellation Orion is called the Horsehead Nebula due to its shape. A particularly bright star shines in the left half of the picture.

of the major signs that help distinguish them from the stars.

Before you go out to watch the stars, always check which planets are in the sky during a given month. You will find this information on pages 117 to 128.

Watching the Sky through Binoculars

All the stars, planets, and other celestial phenomena mentioned in this book are clearly visible to the unaided eye. Celestial bodies that can be seen only through a telescope are not described. But because almost everyone owns a pair of binoculars, a few especially interesting celestial objects that are clearly visible through binoculars are mentioned.

Any ordinary field glasses will do for watching the sky, but they should be held motionless. This is easily done with the help of a photographer's tripod and a small clamp that is attached to the central part of the binoculars. If you try to watch the sky

through handheld binoculars, the normal tremor of your hands is too great, no matter how hard you try to control it, to give you a picture of the stars that does not move. But the use of binoculars mounted on a tripod will open up unexpected possibilities. The increase in the number of stars and other heavenly bodies seen through binoculars versus what the naked-eye observer sees is greater than that yielded by replacing the binoculars with an average-sized telescope.

The Moon is the most important heavenly body on which even small binoculars reveal quite a few features.

Note: The light of the Sun is too brilliant to look into directly, let alone through binoculars. If you looked at the Sun without eye protection, your retinas would be destroyed instantly.

Although most of the heavenly objects described in this book can be viewed with the naked eye, it is highly recommended

The galaxy M 51 in the constellation Canes Venatici (the Hunting Dogs) is 20 million light-years away.

The star cluster the Praesepe, or Beehive, in the constellation Cancer (see page 145).

looking at them at least once with binoculars—except for the Sun, of course. There is just one fact you should be aware of to prevent disappointment: Colors are not discernable, whether you look with the naked eye or through binoculars. Only a few unusually brilliant objects show traces of color; Mars and Betelgeuse, for instance, are slightly reddish; Jupiter looks yellowish, and Sirius is white. All other celestial objects, especially the far away nebulas and galaxies, show up only as tiny, dimly shimmering, unimpressive blurs, even through binoculars. The famous color photos taken at the great observatories were photographed through huge telescopes, sometimes with hour-long exposures, and then underwent complicated photographic processes. Although an attempt is made to show (as well as possible through the Earth's distorting atmosphere) the proper colors, these pictures do not transmit the colors our eyes can perceive directly but reflect various frequencies or wavelengths the objects emit. Long wavelengths appear red, short ones, blue. If you keep all this in mind, you are not likely to experience disappointment when you observe the fascinating night sky.

Star Map Series N I

The map series N I shows the night sky as seen in all countries and cities lying in the latitude between 40 and 60 degrees north.

The farther south you are in this zone, the higher the stars will appear in the southern sky and the lower in the north. Vice versa, the stars will sink lower in the south and be higher in the north as you approach the zone's northerly end at 60 degrees north. The position of the stars relative to each other does not, of course, change.

All the star maps show the night sky as it looks at 11 P.M. at the beginning of the month, at 10 P.M. in the middle of the month, and at 9 P.M. at the end of the month. If daylight saving time is in effect, these times change to midnight, 11 P.M., and 10 P.M., respectively. If you want to watch the sky at another hour, you have to consult the table on page 20.

During the summer months, it does not get dark enough in the countries north of the 55th parallel of latitude for all the stars to become visible. North of the polar circle the Sun is in the sky 24 hours a day.

The star maps N I apply to the following areas and countries: all the northern states of the United States, Canada, Scandinavia, Germany, Belgium, Holland, Luxembourg, Switzerland, northern Italy, France, Great Britain, Poland, Czechoslovakia, Hungary, Romania, Yugoslavia, Bulgaria, and the entire Soviet Union.

What the symbols in the star maps stand for:
-●- = Double stars: Pairs of stars that are particularly close to each other.
◉ = Variable stars: Stars that change in brightness.
☐ = Nebulas: Clouds of gas and dust that shine in colors.
∴ = Star clusters: Aggregations of many stars concentrated in one place.
O = Galaxies: Star systems (the Milky Way is one of many galaxies).

About the brightness and size of the stars marked in the maps:
0 = ☀ The brightest stars. They are easily visible even in big city skies.

1 = ● 2 = ● 3 = ● 4 = • Scale of brightness 0 to 4. The smaller the number, the brighter the star.

◁ *The Andromeda Galaxy is 2.2 million light-years away from us.*

WEST · NORTH · EAST

The evening skies of January offer some of the most beautiful views of the year. In the south, all the winter constellations are gathered. Particularly prominent are Orion, which includes an unusually large number of bright stars, and Sirius, the most brilliant star in the night sky. The Milky Way rises steeply out of the southeast and runs northwest, where, at the constellation Cygnus (the Swan), it dips again below the horizon. The ecliptic, which marks the apparent path of the Sun across the sky, and along which the planets, too, travel, is high in the southern sky, so that in many years the January sky is further adorned by bright planets.

The view to the north is equally interesting. In addition to Ursa Major in the northeast and the clearly visible Great Square of Pegasus, one other constellation stands out. Along with the Big Dipper it is one of the most widely recognized star patterns, namely **Cassiopeia**. Its five stars form an easily spotted W. This striking arrangement of stars gave rise to various imaginative interpretations from earliest times on. It has been taken to depict a hand, a bent leg, and—best known—a sitting female figure, which is in fact the basis of the constellation's present-day name.

In Greek mythology, Cassiopeia was a queen who, together with her husband,

Cepheus, ruled over Ethiopia. They had a daughter, the beautiful Andromeda. Cassiopeia boasted that her daughter was fairer than the Nereids, the daughters of the sea god Poseidon. The Nereids complained of Cassiopeia's arrogance to their father, who sent a sea monster to devastate the coast of Ethiopia. In desperation King Cepheus sent a messenger to the oracle at Delphi for advice. The horrible answer that came back was that Ethiopia would get relief only if Andromeda was sacrificed to the sea monster. Not knowing what else to do, Cepheus and Cassiopeia followed the oracle's advice and chained Andromeda to a rock in the sea. The sea monster was al-

ZENITH

URSA MAJOR
AURIGA
Capella
ε Aur
PERSEUS
Algol
ANDROMEDA

Castor
Pollux
GEMINI
TAURUS
Pleiades
TRIANGULUM

LYNX
M44
Aldebaran
Hyades
ARIES

LEO
CANCER
Betelgeuse
Procyon
ORION
M42
PISCES

CANIS MINOR
Rigel

Regulus
Sirius
Mira

Alphard
CANIS MAJOR
PUPPIS
Adhara
LEPUS
ERIDANUS
CETUS

HYDRA
COLUMBA

EAST   SOUTH   WEST

ready approaching and ready to devour Andromeda when the hero Perseus appeared on the scene. He challenged the monster to battle, and after a long, hard fight he subdued and killed it. He freed Andromeda and brought her back to her parents. Cepheus and Cassiopeia, not knowing how to thank him enough, gave him their daughter in marriage—Andromeda had fallen in love with her savior—and offered all of Ethiopia as a dowry. In commemoration of this great conflict, the gods placed all the participants in the heavens: Next to Cassiopeia and Cepheus we find not only Andromeda and Perseus but also the sea monster in the shape of Cetus, the Whale. The last is visible in January just above the southwestern horizon.

Cassiopeia

WEST   NORTH   EAST

The northern sky is dominated by constellations associated with the stories from Greek mythology that tell about Cassiopeia, Cepheus, Andromeda, and **Perseus**. Perseus was the son of Zeus, the highest of the Greek gods, and Danaë. Because of his partially divine parentage Perseus was able to engage successfully in dangerous adventures, such as the rescuing of Andromeda from the clutches of the sea monster, which appears in the sky as the constellation Cetus (see pages 74–75). Another of his extraordinary deeds was the subduing of Medusa, a horror-inspiring creature, the sight of which turned anyone who beheld her to stone. The Greeks interpreted the constellation Perseus in such a way that the head of Medusa is exactly where the star Algol is, as depicted in the dramatic engraving reproduced from Hevelius's 1690 sky atlas. Algol, also called the demon star, fluctuates in brightness in a regular cycle (see page 130).

The constellations asso-

Perseus

ZENITH

URSA MAJOR

LYNX

AURIGA

Capella

ε Aur

Castor

GEMINI

Algol

PERSEUS

Pollux

M44

CANCER

Pleiades

ARIES

LEO

TAURUS

Aldebaran

Hyades

Regulus

Procyon

Betelgeuse

Denebola

ECLIPTIC

CANIS MINOR

M42

ORION

VIRGO

Alphard

CANIS
MAJOR

Sirius

Rigel

CETUS

HYDRA

PUPPIS

LEPUS

CIRCINUS

Adhara

COLUMBA

ERIDANUS

Mira

EAST   SOUTH   WEST

ciated with the stories about Perseus include a number of other conspicuous celestial objects that are easy to observe in February. The constellation Cepheus, for instance, includes the star Delta Cephei. It, too, is a variable star, although for reasons totally different from those that account for Algol's fluctuations in luminosity. Perseus contains the double star cluster h and χ (chi) Persei, which is a striking sight particularly when viewed through binoculars. Star clusters are collections of many hundred to several thousand stars that are bound together in space by mutual gravitational pull (see page 147).

The most spectacular and interesting celestial object is seen in Andromeda, namely, the great Andromeda Galaxy, M 31. M 31, which was in earlier times thought to be a nebula, is a gigantic galaxy removed from us by the unimaginable distance of 2.2 million light-years (see page 135). On clear nights one can distinctly make out a small, faintly luminous spindle shape (see photo on page 26). Every one of the light rays we perceive has been shooting through space for 2.2 million years before it reaches Earth. You can most easily locate M 31 by first finding the W of Cassiopeia (see January). Then, if you look closely, you can see that the right-hand trough of the W points like a small arrow-head toward M 31.

Over 400 years ago, in the year 1572, an exceptionally brilliant heavenly object turned up in the constellation Cassiopeia. It appeared to be a new star that shone brighter than Venus for several weeks, and it made an impression on the people of the time that is hard to imagine today. The Danish astronomer Tycho Brahe observed the new star especially carefully, which has gone down in history as Tycho's Star. Today we know that a supernova erupted in 1592 in that part of the sky, constituting one of the most gigantic celestial occurrences to have been observed to date (see Lexicon of Celestial Bodies, pages 149–50).

WEST   NORTH   EAST

March ushers in spring in Earth's Northern Hemisphere. It is also the month when daylight saving time starts in many countries. The days now grow longer than the nights and, because the Sun sets later, the stars become visible later.

While the winter constellations, especially Orion, and the star Sirius sink below the horizon early in the evening in the southern sky, in the north **Ursa Major** (the Great Bear), including the seven prominent stars of the Big Dipper—probably the most generally recognized star pattern of the northern sky—assumes its highest and most conspicuous position. The Big Dipper is one of the few names that bear an obvious

relation to the star patterns they refer to. There are four prominent stars that form the bowl or ladle of the Big Dipper; the three other stars are arranged in the slightly bent line and make up the handle. (In Europe the pattern is seen as a plough or a wagon—Charles's Wain.)

The official name of the entire constellation is Ursa Major, the Great Bear or, more accurately, the Great She-Bear. Many different legends are associated with this conspicuous constellation. The best known among them identifies the Great Bear as the nymph Callisto, a beautiful maiden with whom Zeus fell in love. Zeus's wife, the goddess Hera, was so angered that she turned Callisto into a

she-bear and drove her away into the woods of Arcadia. She tormented Callisto so mercilessly that Zeus finally took pity on Callisto and transported her to the heavens as Ursa Major. He placed her far north in the sky so that she became a circumpolar constellation and he could behold her the entire year. What we see as the handle of the Big Dipper is the bear's tail, a rather long one for a bear, as the picture from Hevelius's atlas clearly shows, and quite unlike the short stubs earthly bears sport. In explanation of the elongated tail it is said that Zeus, eager to rescue his sweetheart from Hera's wrath, grabbed her by her nub of a tail and hurled her

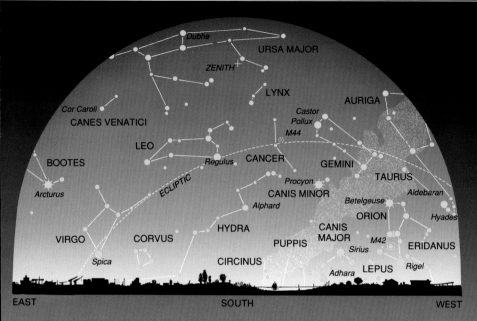

EAST   SOUTH   WEST

into the sky, pulling the tail and thus elongating it.

Ursa Major is of great help in locating other constellations because in the higher northern latitudes it is visible every night (being circumpolar) and because its major stars are easy to recognize when it is still dusk. Draw a mental line between the two stars forming the pouring end of the ladle of the Big Dipper and extend the line five times its length past the star Dubhe. This leads your eye to the North Star, or Polaris (see pages 22–23).

The middle star of the three forming the Dipper's handle (or the Bear's tail) is named Mizar and is especially well known. Right next to it one can make out a somewhat fainter star, Alcor, which was named **Eques Stellula**, or little horseman, in Latin. In this context the Dipper is pictured as a wagon or chariot with Alcor being a small rider perching on the chariot's shaft. Mizar and Alcor also are used to test one's visual acuity because it takes good eyes to see them as two separate stars.

Ursa Major (Big Dipper)

33

WEST   NORTH   EAST

Starting in April, the northern constellations dominate the sky. In the south only three prominent stars are visible: Regulus, Spica, and Arcturus, together sometimes called the Vernal Triangle. Ursa Major and the constellations near it now reach their highest position in the sky, the Great Bear being, in fact, almost exactly at the zenith, directly above the observer's head.

With the help of Ursa Major it is easy to find one of the best known stars of the northern sky, Polaris. Polaris is the most prominent star of Ursa Minor, the Lesser Bear. It stands almost exactly at the north celestial pole and hardly moves at all in the course of the year (see pages 22–23). It is Polaris that Shakespeare refers to when he has Julius Caesar say to the potential murderers surrounding him:

But I am constant as the northern star,/Of whose true-fix'd and resting quality/There is no fellow in the firmament./The skies are painted with unnumb'red sparks,/ They are all fire and every one doth shine;/But

Canes Venatici

there's but one in all doth hold his place./According to modern astronomy, too, Polaris is unusual among the stars. It is a double star or binary, though its companion is visible only through a telescope. Its luminosity fluctuates slightly, and astronomers estimate that the light it emits—at a distance of about 360 light-years—is 1,600 times brighter than that of our Sun. The North Star is thus among the sky's giants.

Another constellation is visible in April high in the sky below the three stars forming the handle of the Big Dipper or the tail of the Great Bear. It is **Canes Venatici** (the Hunting Dogs). This is one of the few constellations seen in the Northern Hemisphere that does not go back to Greek mythology. It was first named around 1650 by Johannes Hevelius, from whose sky atlas the pictures of constellation figures in this book are taken. The brightest star in Canes Venatici is named Cor Caroli, which means Charles's heart. Most names of individual stars, such as Mizar, Alcor, Dubhe, and Arcturus, go back to Arabian astronomers of the first millenium A.D. Cor Caroli is an exception, having been named in 1725 by Edmund Halley, for whom the famous Halley's Comet is named (see pages 133–34). It is said that on May 29, 1660, when King Charles II arrived in London at the restoration of the monarchy af-ter the brief Republican rule of Oliver Cromwell, this star shone especially brightly. However, this is nothing more than pretty popular legend. Cor Caroli has one of the strongest magnetic fields observed to date.

WEST   NORTH   EAST

The night sky changes from month to month. Because the Sun moves through all the constellations of the zodiac in the course of the year (see the zodiac table on page 16), it constantly reveals different stars in a yearly cycle. As the constellations come and go, the position of the Milky Way, too, changes. Thus, in the northern sky, it lies low and parallel to the horizon in May. Visibility has to be especially good for it to be seen at this time of year.

In the southern sky the stars Arcturus, Spica, and Regulus shine forth, forming the Vernal Triangle. Arcturus is the brightest star in the northern half of the sky. It is one of the first stars that can be detected shortly after dusk, and, with the help of the Big Dipper, it is easy to find. If the arc of the Dipper's handle, formed by three stars with Mizar in the middle, is extended across the sky, it leads inevitably to Arcturus, and if the arc is extended even farther, the eye is led to Spica, too.

Arcturus is part of **Boötes** (the Herdsman), a constellation with which several different myths are associated. According to one, Boötes is driving Canes Venatici (the Hunting Dogs), across the sky, chasing them after the Great Bear and the Lesser Bear. Another, prettier story links Boötes to the constellation Virgo (see pages 38–39).

Next to Boötes is the Northern Crown, or Corona Borealis (in the sky of the Southern Hemisphere there is a Southern Crown). This is one of the few instances where no great imagination is required to explain the constellation's name. The Northern Crown's five stars are arranged in a semicircle with one that sparkles especially brightly—named Gemma— in the middle. Gemma, which means "jewel," is 75 light-years distant. It is a so-called spectroscopic binary, that is, a double star whose two components cannot be seen separately even through the most powerful telescope. Only an analysis of its spectrum reveals the star's double nature. The two component

EAST   SOUTH   WEST

stars of Gemma revolve around each other once in 17 days and 12 hours.

The Northern Crown is associated with the myths surrounding Theseus. Theseus accomplished his greatest deed on the island of Crete, where he destroyed the monstrous Minotaur. The Minotaur lived in a labyrinth in the capital city of Crete, and every nine years seven youths and seven virgins had to be sacrificed to it. Theseus decided to kill the Minotaur. Ariadne, the king's daughter, helped him by giving him the famous ball of string. Theseus tied one end of the string to the entrance of the labyrinth and unrolled the ball as he went. Thus, after killing the monster, he was able to find his way out of the labyrinth by following the string. While embarking on this dangerous venture, he wore a crown that the gods had given him and from which shone a brilliant jewel. After slaying the monster, Theseus gave the crown to Ariadne, and later the gods placed it, including Gemma, in the heavens.

Boötes

37

WEST   NORTH   EAST

Starting in June, the visibility of the stars is seriously affected by the onset of summer. The Sun sets so late and twilight persists so long (see Dusk, Midnight Sun, and Polar Night on page 12), that the night is dark enough for watching stars for only about five hours or less.

In the sky, **Virgo** (the Virgin) and Boötes are next to each other, and their stories are bound together in myth, too. In addition to the story claiming that Boötes is herding the bears with his hunting dogs, there is another one. In it, Boötes, the Herdsman, is identified with a mortal named Icarius to whom the gods had presented the gift of wine. Icarius traveled through the countryside with a cart, offering the new beverage to the public. But because they were not familiar with wine, people thought Icarius was trying to poison them and killed him. Only later did they realize what a delightful drink wine was, and then they deeply regretted what they had done. Soon thereafter Icarius's daughter came along looking for her father. When she learned about the sad fate that had befallen him she wept bitter tears, and the gods took pity on both the slain father and his virgin daughter, transforming them into constellations. Even the cart with which the herdsman Icarius had traveled found a place in the heavens as the constellation more generally known as Ursa Minor or the Lesser Bear, which is in this context referred to as the Lesser Wagon. Because Icarius's daughter had carried some ears of wheat in her hand while searching for her father, the brightest star of Virgo is called Spica, which means ear of grain.

As this story about Icarius the Herdsman shows, the constellation now called Ursa Minor was known already among the Greeks as the Lesser Wagon, and, because of its similarity to the Greater Bear, or Greater Wagon, the name Lesser Wagon is sometimes still popularly applied to it in Europe. This group of stars is also the famous Little Dipper. Virgo, with the star Spica, is one of the zodiacal constellations, and the eclip-

EAST   SOUTH   WEST

tic cuts across it. The Moon and all the planets are seen only near the ecliptic and in these constellations (see The Moon and the Planets on page 16).

Spica is an exceptionally radiant star, and it is only because of its great distance from Earth that it is not counted among the brightest stars of the sky. Spica is 300 light-years distant, and its intrinsic luminosity is about 2,300 times greater than the Sun's. It is a so-called spectrographic binary (see page 132), which means that it is really made up of two stars that circle around each other, in this case taking four days for one complete revolution. They are separated from each other by 13 million miles (20 million km), a distance that sounds immense but that shrinks into an angle too small to be measured because the stars are so far removed from us.

Virgo

WEST   NORTH   EAST

In July Earth is at its greatest distance from the Sun (see page 13). The nights are short, and the ecliptic lies low in the south. Consequently the Moon and planets, too, don't rise far above the southern horizon during July. This is why the full moon is always low in the southern sky during summer, whereas in the winter, when the ecliptic is high in the sky, the full moon traverses the firmament more prominently and higher up.

While the ecliptic and, consequently, the constellations of the zodiac are close to the horizon, the Milky Way is all the higher overhead in the summer night sky. The summer months are the best time to observe the Milky Way in the Northern Hemisphere. Today we know that the Milky Way is made up of the combined light of millions of stars, stars that are too faint to be seen individually (see page 140). Before the invention of telescopes, the Milky Way seemed almost like a miraculous object, although many astronomers and thinkers of ancient times suspected its true nature.

There is an old story about the origin and name of the Milky Way that is connected with the famed hero of Greek mythology, **Hercules**. His constellation is in its best viewing position in the sky during the evening hours of July. Hercules was the son of Zeus, but his mother was not Zeus's wife, Hera, but instead the fair mortal Alcmene, daughter of the Mycenean king. Wanting to endow his son with divine strength, Zeus placed the newborn against his sleeping wife's breast, where he could imbibe divine mother's milk. Hercules, however, was so strong even as a baby and sucked so vigorously that the milk spurted way up into the air, rising from Mount Olympus, the abode of the gods, across the sky. The trail it left became the Milky Way. Later on, he performed the 12 Herculean labors as well as other heroic deeds, earning him immortal fame and raising some of his opponents to the status of heavenly constellations as well.

EAST   SOUTH   WEST

The constellation Hercules lies east of Boötes and the Northern Crown (Corona Borealis) and is easiest to find if one looks for the trapezoid formed by the brightest stars at the center of the constellation. To the east of Hercules, in the constellation Cygnus (the Swan), the Milky Way—created according to myth by Hercules—shows a strange feature. It splits into two bands with a dark, starless area between them. This apparent fork in the Milky Way is caused by dark dust clouds that intrude between us and the millions of stars behind them, blocking the light of these stars. The dark clouds of the Milky Way show up dramatically in photographs of the Milky Way and are particularly conspicuous in the constellation Cygnus (see photo, page 140).

Hercules

WEST   NORTH   EAST

Hercules had to perform 12 labors before he was to be permitted to become king of Argos. The victim of his twelfth and last labor is seen in August in a favorable position in the northern sky high above the horizon: It is the constellation **Draco** (the Dragon).

According to Greek myth, a dragon guarded the golden apples of the Hesperides. No one had been strong enough to overcome this dragon until Hercules, after long, errant traveling, arrived at the tree planted by Hera and slew the beast with his gigantic club. He took the apples and brought them back to Eurystheus as proof that he had successfully accomplished the last of his labors. Hera gave the dragon a place in the heavens as a reward for having guarded her tree.

The place for this beast could not have been chosen better, for the stars forming the dragon's body coil through a starless region near the north celestial pole, and the head is marked by four stars next to Hercules. Old representations of the sky's constellations, such as the one in Hevelius's atlas, show the foot of Hercules resting on the conquered beast's head. Hevelius's picture illustrates two other interesting aspects of the constellation. The north pole of the ecliptic is located in Draco. The ecliptic—the apparent path the Sun takes across the sky (see Everything about the Apparent Path

of the Sun, page 15)—has a north and a south pole. This is analagous to the celestial equator and Earth's equator, which have a north and south pole on an axis exactly perpendicular to their plane. In Hevelius's picture, a circle is drawn around the ecliptic north pole in a black-and-white band that runs through the celestial north pole. The distance between the north celestial pole and the ecliptic pole corresponds exactly to the angle by which Earth's axis deviates from the perpendicular of the plane of its orbit around the Sun. The north celestial pole moves around the ecliptic pole describing the circle shown in Hevelius's picture in approximately 26,000 years.

August 1, 11 P.M.
August 15, 10 P.M.
August 31, 9 P.M.

Add one hour if daylight
saving time is in effect.

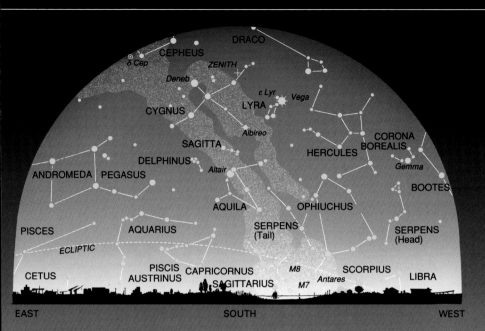

EAST   SOUTH   WEST

Astronomers refer to this important phenomenon as precession, that is, a moving ahead of the celestial pole. This amazing situation, which was recognized in early times by Greek astronomers, accounts for the fact that the north celestial pole slowly moves from constellation to constellation. At the moment it is located at the north or pole star in the constellation Ursa Minor. About 4,000 years ago it lay within Draco, close to a star below the two brightest stars in the Lesser Bear's body (that is, the two outer stars of the bowl of the Little Dipper). In Hevelius's chart, this star is drawn quite prominently. Its name is Thuban. About 5,000 years ago it was the pole star, although it was a rather feeble beacon because it is considerably less bright than Polaris, our present-day North Star.

Draco

WEST   NORTH   EAST

In the Northern Hemisphere, summer officially comes to an end during this month (see page 104). The nights again become longer than the days, and visibility is noticeably improved even during the early evening.

The summer sky is marked for the viewer in the Northern Hemisphere by the Summer Triangle, which is not a constellation but simply a configuration useful for getting oriented. The triangle is made up of Deneb, Altair, and Vega, the brightest stars in the constellations Cygnus, Aquila (the Eagle), and Lyra, respectively. The Summer Triangle is especially helpful because its stars can be perceived quite clearly even in the lit up skies over big cities.

Lyra (the Lyre) and Cygnus (the Swan) are interesting primarily on account of the double stars they contain. Epsilon Lyrae is a double star. It and Mizar-Alcor in Ursa Major (see pages 32–33) are the only binaries whose two component stars are discernable by the unaided eye. Epsilon Lyrae in particular is a real test of eyesight because only someone with extremely sharp vision is able to make out that it is a double star. If you reach for the binoculars, you can tell immediately that Epsilon Lyrae is made up of two stars that are quite far apart from each other. The two stars, also called Epsilon 1 and Epsilon 2, are in turn binaries, but this can be seen only with the aid of a telescope (see page 133).

Cygnus is sometimes referred to as the northern cross because its stars line up in the shape of a cross. It contains the second double star mentioned above, Albireo, but in order to see its two stars separately you need binoculars.

Vega in the constellation Lyra is one of the brightest stars in the northern sky, being almost as brilliant as Arcturus (see page 131). Deneb in the constellation Cygnus looks fainter than Vega, but this is only because Vega is much closer to Earth than Deneb. Vega is a star of normal size, 58 times brighter than the Sun and 26 light-years distant (for more on Vega, see page 151). Deneb,

September 1, 11 P.M.
September 15, 10 P.M.
September 30, 9 P.M.

Add one hour if daylight
saving time is in effect.

EAST   SOUTH   WEST

by contrast, can be described only in superlatives. Astronomers call big stars like Deneb supergiants, and Deneb is, in fact, of gigantic dimensions. Deneb's radiance is at least 60,000 times that of the Sun, and it is 1,600 light-years removed from us, the greatest distance of all the bright stars of the first magnitude. If Deneb were the same distance away from us as Vega is, it would be the brightest star in the sky—16 times brighter even than Venus, presently the most luminous celestial body. It is only the huge distance of 1,600 light-years that makes Deneb's overpowering light output shrink to a moderate brightness that is comparable to that of stars located much closer to us. The only reason why all the stars in the sky appear to us equidistant is that our senses and mind are incapable of perceiving or comprehending the astronomic distances involved.

Cygnus

WEST   NORTH   EAST

In October, the Summer Triangle can be seen in the west during the early evening hours. The constellations Lyra, Cygnus, and Aquila, which contain the stars making up the Summer Triangle, also go back to Greek mythology. The lyre was the instrument played so beautifully by the famous singer Orpheus that even the stones were moved to weep. Cygnus is usually associated with the story of Leda and the swan. Leda was a beautiful mortal with whom the god Zeus fell in love. Because Leda loved her husband and was true to him, Zeus approached her in the guise of a swan. Leda, who did not recognize Zeus, entered the water with him, and from their union beautiful Helen was born, on whose account the Trojan War was fought. In 1975 a new star or nova rose to brightness in Cygnus and could be seen easily by the unaided eye for several weeks, even making headlines in the newspapers. **Aquila** (the Eagle) was sent by Zeus to sweep up the youth Antinous and bring him up

Aquila

EAST   SOUTH   WEST

to Olympus, where he became cupbearer for the gods. As an expression of gratitude the gods originally placed both the eagle and Antinous among the stars, and in Hevelius's atlas both figures appear together. But as a consequence of an overall revision of the constellations that became effective in 1930, Antinous has vanished from today's sky.

South of Cygnus there are two small constellations. One of them, Delphinus (the Dolphin), is very easy to spot. Its four brightest stars form an easily recognizable trapezoid. The other one is Sagitta (the Arrow), one of the smallest of all the constellations. The dolphin, according to legend, helped Poseidon find lovely Amphitrite, whom the sea god had long been looking for in vain. In his gratitude, Poseidon transformed the dolphin into a heavenly constellation. The arrow, finally, is said to have been used by Hercules to kill an eagle that was tormenting Orpheus. (This is obviously a different story from the one in which the eagle is connected with the boy Antinous.)

The brightest star in Aquila (the Eagle) is Altair. It takes only 6½ hours to spin once around its axis (our Sun takes 25½ days; see pages 149–50). Altair is 16 light-years away from Earth (that amounts to roughly 100 trillion miles or 160 trillion km) and is thus one of our Sun's closer neighbors. Much more spectacular than Altair was Nova Aquilae, a nova that burst forth in great brightness in June of 1918, lending Aquila a very different look for several weeks as it grew more luminous than Sirius, the brightest star in the sky. Novas (new stars) are sudden outbursts of light in previously obscure stars. These dramatic surges are due to profound changes in the physical processes going on in the stars (see pages 142–43).

47

WEST   NORTH   EAST

The approach of winter becomes apparent during November not only in the air but in the sky as well. In the evening, Orion, the constellation typical of the winter sky, already can be seen in the east. Above Orion we find, clearly visible, **Auriga** (the Charioteer) and Taurus (the Bull), two more winter constellations. To be sure, Auriga has been quite apparent in the sky for some months; in fact, Capella, its brightest star, is circumpolar and thus can be seen throughout the year (see page 23).

Capella is one of the ten brightest stars in the sky (see page 133). Capella, which means little she-goat, usually is depicted in old renditions of the starry sky as sitting on the shoulder of the charioteer, who holds a whip. At this point in time it is difficult to understand just what the connection between the charioteer and the little goat originally was. A number of sometimes mutually contradictory stories surround the figure of the charioteer.

According to one of these stories, the charioteer was Phaeton, the son of the sun god Helios. Helios drove across the sky every day in a fiery chariot, providing light for Earth. But only he could control the powerful horses that pulled the chariot. When Phaeton, going against his father's express prohibition, tried to drive the chariot, he lost control of the horses and tumbled from the sky.

The course the plunging, careening chariot took is said to have formed the Milky Way—a totally different explanation from that offered by the legend that tells of milk spurting across the sky from Hera's breast (see page 40).

In another myth Auriga, the charioteer, represents Hephaestus, the god of fire and iron forging. He invented the four-horse chariot and, as a reward, was transformed into a constellation.

Auriga appears in the sky as a figure made up by four stars. Usually a fifth star to the south is included even though the exact delineation of the constellations reflecting modern revisions assigns it to Taurus. That is why this

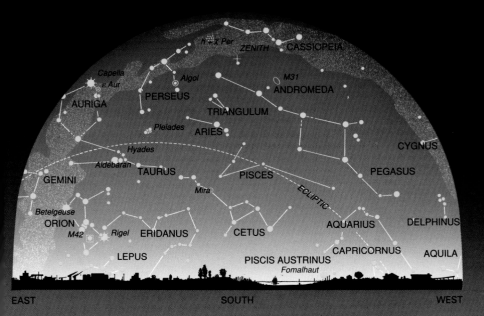

star is connected to the rest of Auriga with dotted lines. In addition to bright Capella, Auriga contains another remarkable star, Epsilon Aurigae. It is a variable star of huge dimensions, one of the largest and most mysterious variables known (see pages 150–51).

Every November a shower of meteors is seen, the so-called Leonid meteors. They appear in the middle of the month, and approximately every 33 years there is an unusually large number of them (see page 139). The Leonids all seem to radiate from the constellation Leo (the Lion). Leo does not appear in November's sky charts because it does not become visible until early morning, around 2 A.M., and different charts apply for that time (see table, page 20).

Auriga

PERSEUS
Algol
TRIANGULUM
ε Aur
ZENITH
Capella
h + χ Per
M31
AURIGA
ANDROMEDA
CASSIOPEIA
GEMINI
Castor
Pollux
δ Cep
Polaris
CEPHEUS
URSA MINOR
CANCER
Dubhe
M44
PEGASUS
URSA MAJOR
Deneb
LYNX
DRACO
ECLIPTIC
Mizar
CYGNUS
Alcor
LEO
LYRA
DELPHINUS
ε Lyr Vega
HERCULES
Albireo
Cor Caroli
CANES VENATICI
Regulus

WEST   NORTH   EAST

December marks the beginning of winter in the Northern Hemisphere. In the evening all the winter constellations are gathered in the east, and their brightest stars combine in a large hexagon, the Winter Hexagon. The corners are made up by the stars Rigel in Orion, Sirius in Canis Major, Procyon in Canis Minor, Castor and Pollux in Gemini, Capella in Auriga, and Aldebaran in Taurus.

Aldebaran belongs to the groups of red giants (distance: 68 light-years; diameter: 40 times that of the Sun) and appears reddish in the midst of the Hyades star cluster, which it is not, however, part of. Farther north is the Pleiades star cluster. It is part of the constellation **Taurus**.

The Hyades and the Pleiades are the most conspicuous and famous of the star clusters (see pages 135, 145, and 147).

Aldebaran is one of the major reasons why the constellation Taurus was conceived, for not only the Greeks but many other early people thought they could see a powerful beast in this group of stars, with reddish Aldebaran forming its eye. Aldebaran, along with Spica in the constellation Virgo (see pages 38–39), is one of the few bright stars that can be eclipsed by the Moon. This is possible because Aldebaran stands immediately next to the ecliptic, the apparent path the Sun follows across the sky.

The most famous of the eclipses of Aldebaran took place in the year A.D. 509. It was visible from Athens and gave rise, 1,200 years later, in the early days of modern astronomy, to an important discovery. In 1735, Edmund Halley reconstructed the course of the Moon far back into the past. He found to his amazement that according to his calculations Aldebaran could not have been eclipsed by the Moon in A.D. 509— Aldebaran would have had to be farther to the south. This inspired Halley's idea— a true stroke of genius considering the time when he conceived it—that Aldebaran might have changed position in the course of almost 1,200 years. Halley was thus the first to discover that the

EAST   SOUTH   WEST

so-called fixed stars are not stationary. In fact, the stars only seem to adhere to their places in the sky. We get that impression because they are so astronomically far away from us. The stars' remoteness makes the vast distances they travel shrink into angles that are too small to measure. All stars are in motion, but their movement is discernable only by means of precise measurements or through observation over a very long time span—over 1,000 years in Halley's case. The movement of the stars has produced no visible changes in the sky since the Greeks scanned it. But in 100,000 years or so the sky as we know it today is likely to have a dramatically different aspect because of the the stars' proper motion, which was first recognized in Aldebaran. If we saw the sky after such a lapse of time, the constellations would have undergone such profound changes that their names would have lost all meaning.

Taurus

Star Map Series N II

The stars shown in series N II can be seen between the 20th and 40th degrees of northern latitude. The geographic map below shows the exact position of this latitudinal zone. These star maps therefore depict the skies that people living in the northern part of the world would see on vacation trips to the south. Here the constellations of Earth's Southern Hemisphere begin to become clearly visible above the horizon, constella-tions such as Centaurus (star maps N II/5 and 6) and Carina (star map N II/2).

The ecliptic, the apparent circle described by the Sun on the celestial sphere, is higher in the sky than in the maps of series N I. This means, too, that the planets look more dramatic and stay in the sky longer (see pages 16 and 113). It is also night earlier, especially in the southern parts of zone N II, because the Sun sets faster and dusk is brief.

The star maps N II apply in the following countries and areas: the southern parts of the United States, Mexico, the Caribbean, Cuba, Spain, Portugal, southern Italy, Greece, Turkey, Israel, Egypt, Tunisia, Algeria, Morocco, Persia, Pakistan, Afghanistan, Saudi Arabia, India, Thailand, Burma, China, Korea, Japan, and Taiwan.

What the symbols in the star maps stand for:

● = Double stars: Pairs of stars that are particularly close to each other.

◉ = Variable stars: Stars that change in brightness.

□ = Nebulas: Clouds of gas and dust that shine in colors.

∴ = Star clusters: Aggregations of many stars concentrated in one place.

O = Galaxies: Star systems (the Milky Way is one of many galaxies).

About the brightness and size of the stars marked in the maps:

0 = ☀ The brightest stars. They are easily visible even in big city skies.

1 = ● 2 = ● 3 = ● 4 = • Scale of brightness 0 to 4. The smaller the number, the brighter the star.

The Great Nebula in Orion is a gas cloud that is 1,500 light-years distant from us.

Today 88 constellations are recognized. It is easy to list them in order of size and position, but it is harder to say which constellation is the most magnificent. Still, most stargazers probably would agree that this rank should go to a constellation that shows up prominently high in the southern sky in January, namely **Orion.**

Orion is the only constellation that includes not just one but two of the sky's ten brightest stars: Betelgeuse (see page 131) and Rigel (see page 146). The rest of Orion's stars are also among the brighter ones and make up an impressive configuration in the sky. Three of them are arranged in a straight line or belt in the middle, with two stars each above and below the belt. From the dawn of human civilization, people who gazed up at the sky trying to interpret it thought they could recognize in this star pattern a gigantic figure: a hunter or a warrior, with Betelgeuse marking one shoulder and, in the lower half, Rigel together with its somewhat dimmer companion forming the knee or foot.

In keeping with his celestial grandeur, Orion is described in Greek mythology as an exceptionally mighty hunter. Usually he is depicted with his shield facing west to ward off the powerful bull (Taurus) and, with the other hand, swinging a club in the same direction. But the myths tell not only of Orion's con-tests with wild animals and human opponents but also of his interest in beautiful maidens. Thus he kept chasing after the Pleiades, the seven daughters of the giant Atlas, until they begged Zeus to save them from Orion's pursuits. Zeus responded by moving not only the Pleiades but Orion as well to the heavens, where the latter is forced to follow them without ever being able to catch up as they precede him across the sky from east to west. In another legend Orion is said to have made advances to Artemis, which also angered the gods. They sent a scorpion after him to sting him with its deadly poison. Just as Orion collapsed, Asclepius, the god of healing, happened to

EAST   SOUTH   WEST

come by and tried to save Orion. But the gods' wrath was so great that Zeus hurled a bolt of lightning down at Orion as a final punishment. The lightning also killed Asclepius. All three earthly participants were turned into constellations. Asclepius appears in the sky under the name of Ophiuchus (the Serpent Bearer). The gods placed the constellations so ingeniously that the three never meet in the sky. Ophiuchus shows up there at a season when Orion becomes invisible (see stars in July, pages 66–67), and Scorpius is on the opposite side of the celestial sphere from Orion.

In addition to forming a striking pattern and having many bright stars, Orion also includes a number of other famous celestial objects, such as the Great Nebula in Orion, M 42. This is a gigantic, brightly shining gas cloud, which counts among the most colorful and notable celestial sights of this kind (see page 142).

Orion

55

Aldebaran
TAURUS
Hyades
ε Aur Capella
Pleiades
PERSEUS
ARIES
Algol
TRIANGULUM
h + χ Per
ANDROMEDA
CASSIOPEIA
PISCES M31
δ Cep
ECLIPTIC

Pollux
Castor ZENITH
GEMINI
AURIGA
URSA MAJOR
Dubhe
Polaris URSA MINOR
Alcor Mizar
CEPHEUS
DRACO

M44
CANCER
Regulus
LYNX
LEO
Denebola
Cor Caroli
CANES VENATICI
BOOTES VIRGO
Arcturus

WEST   **NORTH**   **EAST**

In keeping with the time of year, the typical winter constellations dominate the sky in February. Sirius, the brightest star in the sky, is in its highest possible position over the horizon, almost due south. Because of its outstanding brightness it always has been an object of greatest interest, and there is hardly a star around which as many stories are woven—and which has given rise to as many interesting scientific discoveries—as Sirius (see also pages 146–47).

Sirius is part of the constellation **Canis Major** (the Greater Dog). Somewhat higher in the sky we find Canis Minor (the Lesser Dog), which consists practically of one star only, Procyon, an-

other one of the ten brightest stars in the sky (see page 145). In most star legends, the two constellations are regarded together as the dogs of the celestial hunter Orion. There is also, however, a story in which Canis Minor figures together with Boötes and Virgo (see pages 36–37). The expression dog days, which refers to the hottest period of

Canis Major

56

summer in August, derives from Canis Major. Canis Major is a winter constellation. In the months following February this constellation moves more and more westward in the evening until the Sun, traveling along the path of the ecliptic, is so close to it that it disappears from view as Canis Major accompanies the Sun across the daytime sky. This is the case in June and July. By August the Sun has moved farther along, and Canis Major makes its first brief appearance again in the dawn just before sunrise. After that it rises a little bit earlier every day, like all the stars, and in winter it can be seen in the evening sky again.

This first rise of Canis Major in the morning after a prolonged absence is more apparent than that of other constellations because Sirius, the brightest star, is easy to spot. That is why Sirius and Canis Major long ago became a symbol for the hottest days of summer, the dog days. Sirius even played a role of special importance in the calendar and daily life of ancient Egypt. The reason for this is that at the time around 3000 B.C. the first reappearance in the sky of Sirius coincided with the flooding of the Nile. These yearly floods were crucial for plentiful harvests, and thus Sirius, under the name of Sothis, was venerated as a god.

Sirius, which is one of the first stars to appear in the sky after sunset, serves as a lode-star even today. Next to it the other stars comprising Canis Major pale, even though they include a number of remarkable stars. Especially worth mentioning is Adhara, which is next in brightness within the constellation. It is 900 times more radiant than the Sun but is 500 light-years away. That is the only reason why it appears fainter to us than its bigger brother, Sirius, which is removed only 8.7 light-years from Earth.

57

WEST   NORTH   EAST

Beginning in March, the month that ushers in spring, the winter constellations are in the western sky in the evening. They sink below the horizon around midnight. This is the last time until the following winter that the Winter Hexagon can be seen, this hexagon in which are gathered six stars belonging to some of the most beautiful constellations: Capella in Auriga; Aldebaran in Taurus; Rigel in Orion; Sirius in Canis Major; Procyon in Canis Minor; and, finally, Castor or Pollux in Gemini.

It is not altogether clear which of the twins should be included in the hexagon because they are more or less equally luminous and stand so close to each other that the

name **Gemini** (the Twins) comes to mind quite automatically. In Greek mythology, from which the names Castor and Pollux come, the twins have different fathers. The story is that Zeus became infatuated with beautiful Leda, who loved her husband truly. So Zeus changed himself into a swan and visited her. Leda, who suspected nothing, made love with her husband that same night, and thus she came to bear male twins who had different fathers. Pollux was the son of Zeus and therefore immortal, whereas his brother, Castor, was an ordinary mortal. The brothers loved each other dearly and performed many heroic deeds together. Eventually Castor died, and Pol-

lux asked Zeus to make him mortal, too. Zeus refused to grant this wish, and so Pollux decided to follow his brother into the underworld. Deeply impressed by such profound brother love, Zeus moved both of them into the heavens. Modern astronomers view these two stars in a very different light with no sign of brotherhood between them. Pollux is 35 light-years away from us, Castor, 50 light-years. Pollux is a single star, while Castor is made up of six stars that form one of the most unusual multiple star systems in the sky.

Gemini is one of the zodiacal constellations through which the Sun progresses. When it reaches Gemini, the Sun is in its highest position

EAST · SOUTH · WEST

in the sky as seen from Earth's Northern Hemisphere. The fact that Gemini belongs to the zodiacal constellations is also the reason why two of the three major planets that are visible only through a telescope were first discovered in this constellation. In 1781 the astronomer William Herschel, observing the sky from England, first saw Uranus, and in 1930 the American Clyde Tombaugh discovered Pluto, also in Gemini.

Cancer (the Crab), also a zodiacal constellation, is next to Gemini to the east. It and Libra are the least conspicuous constellations of the zodiac. Cancer is said to have been crushed underfoot in the course of Hercules's battle with Hydra (the Water Snake) (see pages 62–63). The luckless crab nevertheless was raised to the heavens by the mother goddess Hera. Cancer's claim to fame is based primarily on the open star cluster M 44, which is one of the brightest in the sky and often is referred to as the Praesepe (Latin for manger) or the Beehive (see page 145).

Gemini

59

Denebola

LEO   ZENITH

Regulus

ECLIPTIC

Cor Caroli

CANCER   CANES VENATICI   Arcturus

URSA MAJOR

M44

LYNX   Mizar Alcor   BOOTES

Pollux   Dubhe   Gemma

Castor   DRACO   CORONA
                                                 BOREALIS
GEMINI   SERPENS
                        URSA MINOR   (Head)

                        Polaris   HERCULES

         AURIGA
              Capella   CEPHEUS
CANIS   ε Aur   Vega   OPHIUCHUS
MINOR   h + χ   ε Lyr
Procyon   PERSEUS   Per   LYRA
      TAURUS   CASSIOPEIA   CYGNUS   LYRA

WEST   NORTH   EAST

To get oriented in the night sky, many observers look not only for the constellations shown in the sky charts but also resort to other star combinations to help them get their bearings. Thus there is a Winter Hexagon, an Autumn Square (the Great Square of Pegasus), a Summer Triangle, and a Vernal Triangle to look for. The Vernal Triangle stands especially high and prominent in the southern sky during April, the first month that belongs entirely to spring. The triangle is made up of the brightest stars in the constellations Boötes, Virgo, and Leo.

The brightest star in Leo is named Regulus, which means little king. **Leo** (the Lion) is one of the constella-

tions that is easy to spot in the sky because it is made up of two easy to recognize trapezoids. The lower, larger trapezoid has Regulus and the next brightest star, Denebola, as its bottom corners, and the smaller trapezoid sits atop the bigger one to one side. It doesn't take a great deal of imagination to see the head and body of a mighty lion in this arrangement of stars, and it is not surprising that the name Leo, as applied to this area of the sky, is of great antiquity. Leo is associated with one of the great feats of Hercules, whose constellation appears in the April sky, too, in the east. Hercules's first labor was to slay the Nemean lion, a fearful beast whose skin was im-

mune to all injury, so that Hercules could not subdue the animal with either bow and arrow or a club. He therefore grabbed it by the throat and choked it to death. Then he skinned the dead lion and wore its pelt as a fear-inspiring garment. But because the Nemean lion was an immortal animal, the gods brought it back to life as a constellation in the heavens.

Leo is one of the zodiacal constellations along the ecliptic. Regulus, its brightest star, stands almost on the exact line of the ecliptic and thus is obscured periodically by the Moon. It is even possible for planets to come between it and Earth, so that its light rays are blocked. But because the planets appear

EAST   SOUTH   WEST

so much smaller on Earth than does the broad face of the Moon, this happens only very infrequently. The only time this kind of celestial event has been observed since the beginning of modern astronomy was on July 7, 1959, when Venus covered up Regulus. Regulus is 80 light-years away from Earth and is 160 times more radiant than the Sun. Its diameter is estimated to be five times that of the Sun.

The second brightest star in Leo, Denebola, further reaffirms the name given by astronomers to this region of the sky. It comes from the Arabic and means lion's tail. Denebola is of medium size. It is 40 light-years away and about 20 times brighter than the Sun.

Leo

WEST   NORTH   EAST

Because the Sun sets later at this time of year, the visibility of the stars is noticeably lessened. Dusk lasts longer, so it is not until about 10 P.M. (11 P.M. where daylight saving time is in effect) that the constellations can be made out.

The paucity of bright stars is particularly striking in the lower half of the southern sky, where a surprisingly large celestial expanse contains only one constellation, Hydra. **Hydra** (the Water Snake) is the largest of the 88 officially recognized constellations, but its stars are much fainter than those of the smallest constellation, the Southern Cross, which is invisible from the 30th degree of northern latitude. The long drawn out body of Hydra has only one fairly bright star, Alphard. The name is fitting in view of the faintness of Hydra. It translates as the solitary one, that is, it is the only star to draw the eye's attention in an otherwise starless region of the sky. Alphard shines with a slightly reddish light and is 90 light-years away from Earth.

Hydra is connected to the myths about Hercules and his famous 12 labors. After Hercules had vanquished the lion, whose constellation is also visible in May in the southwestern sky, his next task was to slay the Hydra. This monster was especially terrifying because it had seven heads, and for every head that was cut off, new ones grew back instantly in its place. Thus Hercules found himself in serious straits until Athene helped him with some advice. On her suggestion he now asked his nephew, who had accompanied him, to hand him flaming torches with which he cauterized each stump after a head was severed and thus prevented the sprouting of new ones. When Hera, Hercules's arch enemy, saw that he was about to triumph after all, she sent the crab after him at the last moment to bite him, but Hercules crushed it underfoot, whereupon it was turned into the constellation Cancer.

On a clear night, once it is dark enough, the whole body of the Hydra can be made out. The brighter stars, which

62

EAST   SOUTH   WEST

are shown in the chart, form a snakelike line across the sky. The head, indicated by two somewhat brighter stars than most of the rest, is next to Cancer. Many other con- stellations show up more faintly in the May sky in late evening. In the north there are Cepheus and Lynx. The lynx, about which there is not much to report, was defined by Johannes Hevelius, who gave it its present name be- cause, supposedly, one had to have "the eyes of a lynx" to make out the faint stars of this constellation.

Hydra

June
Star map N II/6

SERPENS (Head)

Arcturus

Gemma

ZENITH

CORONA
BOREALIS

BOOTES

HERCULES

LYRA AQUILA

Cor Caroli

Vega

ε Lyr

Albireo

CANES VENATICI

Alcor
Mizar

DRACO

Denebola

SAGITTA Altair

Deneb

ECLIPTIC

Dubhe

LEO

Polaris

URSA MINOR

CYGNUS DELPHINUS

CEPHEUS

δ Cep

Regulus

LYNX

URSA MAJOR

CANCER

CASSIOPEIA

PEGASUS

WEST NORTH EAST

June marks the beginning of summer. Everywhere in the Northern Hemisphere the Sun now stands highest in the sky; the days are longer than at any other time of the year, and the nights are shorter, although all this is not as pronounced between the 30th and 40th degrees of northern latitude as it is farther north (see What Causes the Seasons of the Year? on page 13). Just like May, June is a month of rather inconspicuous constellations that are seldom mentioned but that nevertheless display a number of interesting features.

Due south and on the ecliptic we find Libra. **Libra** (the Scales) is the only constellation of the zodiac that is not named after an animal

or a person. The name Libra has direct reference to the movement of the Sun. Originally this constellation was considered part of Scorpius, with the two brightest stars

making up the claws of the scorpion. But very early, and probably originating in Egypt, the name Libra gained currency because the Sun passes through Libra at the

Libra

64

EAST   SOUTH   WEST

time of the fall equinox in September, when day and night are of equal length. After the equinox, the Sun begins to sink lower in the sky until winter begins. The scales, which stand as a symbol for balance and justice, thus seemed an obvious candidate to mark this special position of the Sun in the sky, especially the equality of day and night in the fall, when winter is still distant but the hot days of summer are clearly past. As is the case with the other constellations of the zodiac, planets frequently show up in Libra (see The Planets Appear in the Constellations of the Zodiac on page 113).

Next to Libra on the ecliptic, to the east, is Scorpius, which also belongs to the zodiac. On the west, Libra is preceded by Virgo and Leo. South of Virgo is the constellation Corvus (the Crow), whose origins are obscure. We do know that it goes back to the Greeks, but the legends associated with it are contradictory. According to one of them, the crow was sent by Apollo to fetch water from a spring. But the crow found some delicious figs on the way and stopped to eat them. When he returned, he was clutching the water snake in his claws and claimed he had found no water because the snake had drunk the spring empty. Apollo, realizing immediately that this was a lie, banished the crow to the heavens, along with the Hydra, where he is condemned to suffer eternal thirst.

Because in June the sky is so bright before midnight, it is especially important to remember how to get one's bearings by first finding the Big Dipper in Ursa Major. Ursa Major is in the northeast during June. Once the characteristic pattern of the Big Dipper is identified it is not difficult to find Boötes, Virgo, and Cassiopeia, as well as many other constellations.

In July, the distance between the Sun and Earth grows largest. We have hot summer weather in spite of this because of the tilt of Earth's axis, which results in the Sun passing through the sky in a high arc during the day and thus shining longer (see pages 12–13). The ecliptic, the apparent path of the Sun across the celestial sphere, is consequently very low in the southern sky during July evenings and nights, and whatever planets appear are close to the horizon, too.

But the southern part of the sky is particularly interesting on account of the constellations that show up there. Sagittarius, Scorpius, and Ophiuchus are all there, and the Milky Way passes through them, being brightest in Sagittarius because the center of the galaxy lies in that direction (see pages 92–93). All three constellations mentioned are part of the zodiac, but **Ophiuchus** (the Serpent Bearer) is the one that requires comment because it is the thirteenth zodiacal constellation. In the classical zodiac that is still used today in horoscopes, there is no serpent bearer. Ophiuchus was not included among the zodiacal constellations until 1930, when the boundaries of the constellations were revised (see page 16).

The serpent bearer is closely linked to **Serpens** (the Snake or Serpent). In old representations of the starry skies, Ophiuchus is shown holding the snake in his hands, and the modern redefinition of the constellations still adheres to this old interpretation. Serpens is the only constellation that consists of two separate parts, namely the head and the tail. This means that though there are 88 constellations, the sky is divided into 89 sections because the snake consists of two unconnected segments.

The snake and the snake bearer are associated in Greek mythology with the god of healing, Asclepius. Even today a snake wound around a staff is the symbol of medicine and pharmacology. Asclepius was a renowned physician. In fact, he practiced his art so successfully that he eventually aroused the ire of Pluto, the god of the underworld, who complained to Zeus that not enough mortals were arriving in his realm anymore. Zeus thereupon struck Asclepius with a bolt of lightning. In another tale Asclepius tried to save the mortally wounded Orion, whereupon he suffered the same fate.

In 1604 Ophiuchus was the site of the eruption of a supernova. This was the last such blaze that could be seen with the naked eye. One astronomer who watched with special closeness was Johannes Kepler, and it became known as Kepler's Star. This supernova in Ophiuchus was visible for 18 months and both fascinated and alarmed the people of the early seventeenth century because only 30 years earlier another supernova had erupted in Cassiopeia (which can be found in the northern sky in July). At the height of its blaze, the supernova in Ophiuchus was brighter than Jupiter (see pages 149–50).

Ophiuchus and Serpens

AQUILA SAGITTA DELPHINUS
Albireo ZENITH
LYRA CYGNUS
Vega ε Lyr
HERCULES Deneb PEGASUS
CEPHEUS
CORONA DRACO δ Cep
Gemma BOREALIS CASSIOPEIA
SERPENS ANDROMEDA
(Head) M31
BOOTES Polaris
Alcor URSA MINOR PISCES
Arcturus Mizar h + χ Per
URSA MAJOR TRIANGULUM
Cor Caroli Dubhe PERSEUS ECLIPTIC
CANES VENATICI Algol
ARIES

WEST   NORTH   EAST

During the hottest month in Earth's Northern Hemisphere, the Summer Triangle stands out clearly overhead. It is made up of the brightest stars of Cygnus, Lyra, and Aquila, namely Deneb, Vega, and Altair. Low on the northeastern horizon, Perseus rises with its double cluster h and χ (chi) and the famous variable star Algol.

Perseus is also the site, or radiant, of the most spectacular meteor shower of the year, the Perseids. Around August 10, large numbers of meteors seem to stream from this constellation. At this time of year, Earth traverses an exceptionally dense accumulation of dust particles that enter Earth's atmosphere where they heat up the air and create the familiar light streaks we call meteors or shooting stars (see page 138). The best time to watch for the Perseids is after midnight because Perseus stands higher in the sky then. The Moon should interfere as little as possible and therefore not be in its full phase (see table on pages 106–107).

Scorpius

EAST   SOUTH   WEST

In the south, the Milky Way is prominently visible because it rises almost vertically from the horizon to the zenith. Along the way it passes through an interesting constellation, namely **Scorpius**, which is one of the zodiacal constellations (see page 16). Scorpius, too, is of ancient origin, and it includes a number of resplendent stars, including Antares, the brightest in this constellation. Antares is one of the few stars that shows a clear color. It shines with a reddish light, to which it owes its name. Because Mars is red—like Antares—and because, as a planet, Mars also moves along the ecliptic and therefore appears in Antares's vicinity with some frequency,

it was dubbed anti-Mars, for Ares was the Greek god of war, known to the Romans as Mars.

Antares is so close to the ecliptic that it often is hidden by the Moon. It is an unusual star about 500 light-years away. Astronomers term it a supergiant—like Betelgeuse in Orion (see pages 131 and 55). Its diameter exceeds that of our Sun by 700 times. If it were located where the Sun is, it would extend beyond the orbit of Mars and swallow Earth up completely. Its light is at least 7,600 times brighter than that of the Sun. Also in Scorpius the open star cluster M 7 is found, one of the few clusters visible to the naked eye (see pages 147–49).

The story of Scorpius is closely linked to those of some of the other constellations. Thus, according to one myth, Scorpius mortally stung Orion (see page 55) and was placed in the heavens in such a way that it and Orion are always on opposite sides of the sky and consequently never meet. Scorpius is a summer constellation, whereas Orion appears only in winter.

WEST   NORTH   EAST

September marks the beginning of fall. Day and night are of approximately equal length (see pages 12–13 and 104–05), so that the stars are again easier to watch because they show up earlier in the evening.

This is important because now many of the familiar constellations are low on the horizon in the evening and only relatively faint stars occupy the better positions in the sky. Ursa Major, for instance, is extremely low in the north—so low, in fact, that in this southerly latitude some of its stars have sunk below the horizon. The ecliptic is about half way up in the sky in the south, where it transects Capricornus and **Aquarius** (the Water Bearer).

Both these constellations consequently often form the backdrop for planets, which also can be observed easily in September. In September of 1846, the planet Neptune, one of the three planets that are not visible to the naked eye, was first detected in the constellation Capricornus.

Capricornus and Aquarius lend themselves particularly well to illustrate an important phenomenon in the movement of the stars. On many geographical maps, the term Tropic of Capricorn is used even today to indicate the parallel of latitude at 23½ degrees south of the equator. Every year when the Sun is at this southern limit of its annual path, that is, at the beginning of winter in the

Northern Hemisphere, it appears exactly on the zenith at noon, that is, directly overhead. In the time before Christ's birth when these ancient concepts were formed, the Sun stood among the stars of Capricornus at this time of year. This no longer is true today; it now stands in the constellation Sagittarius at the beginning of winter, and it therefore would be more accurate now to speak of a Tropic of Sagittarius.

This shift is due to the same phenomenon that also accounts for the changing position of the north celestial pole (see the constellation Draco, on pages 42–43). It is called precession, that is, the gradual moving ahead of the most important lines and

EAST   SOUTH   WEST

points of orientation—the celestial equator and the celestial poles—against the background of the stars. Once in the course of 26,000 years these lines and points describe a complete circle in the celestial sphere. Since the naming of the Tropic of Capricorn, the lowest point the Sun reaches on the ecliptic has moved from Capricornus to Sagittarius; and the spot where it always stands at the beginning of spring, known as the vernal equinox, has moved similarly out of Aries and into Pisces. Because of this new position, astrology calls the present time the Age of Pisces. But because the vernal equinox keeps moving along the ecliptic, it will enter the constellation Aquarius around the year 2400. Then the Age of Aquarius will begin, when—the story goes—everything on Earth will be better and more peaceful. This is the astronomical background of the popular song "The Age of Aquarius" from the world famous musical *Hair*.

Aquarius

Every season of the year has its typical constellations. Because, in its apparent motion, the Sun completes a circle around the celestial sphere in the course of a year, different stars are seen at night from month to month, stars that six months later cross the daytime sky along with the Sun, invisible because of the bright sunlight. It is thus the Sun that determines, with its apparent movement, which stars are visible during which part of the year, whereas Earth's rotation around its own axis accounts for the fact that individual stars are visible in different places at different hours of the night (see The Movement of Earth on page 8).

The night sky therefore looks the same at a given season every year, except for the position of the planets (see pages 113–17). In the fall, the Autumn Square, also called the Great Square of Pegasus, is particularly conspicuous. It is formed by four stars from the constellations **Pegasus** and Andromeda and stands directly overhead in October, in the highest point of the sky, the zenith.

The constellation of Pegasus usually is represented by this almost perfect square, even though the star forming one of its corners is part of Andromeda. This usually is indicated in star maps by dotted lines. Pegasus is named after a famous legendary beast of Greek mythology, a winged horse. Pegasus was born from the blood of the Gorgon Medusa, who was so terrible to behold that anyone who laid eyes on her instantly turned to stone. When Perseus set out to conquer her, he had the foresight not to look at her directly but only at her reflection on his shield. In this way he was able to overcome her. When he finally killed her, Pegasus sprang forth from the severed head, spread his wings, and flew up to the gods in the heavens. Perseus, Andromeda, Cepheus, and Cassiopeia all figure together in Greek mythology and are all visible in the northern sky during October.

Pegasus went on to perform many heroic deeds at

EAST   SOUTH   WEST

he behest of the gods. At one point, when he landed on the island Helion, he struck the ground with his hooves and caused the fountain of wisdom to flow. Anyone who drank from this spring was filled with poetic imagination, so that Pegasus later became a symbol of poetry.

The constellation Pegasus extends far beyond its Great Square, reaching as far as Cygnus and Delphinus in the west. In spite of its size, Pegasus contains very few remarkable stars or unusual celestial objects. The opposite is true of Andromeda, which displays the famous Andromeda Galaxy, one of the few galaxies visible to the naked eye (see page 135). Its official designation is M 31, which means that it is the thirty-first entry in the catalog compiled by Charles Messier in the eighteenth century. Altogether, the view into the north yields more during October than does the southern sky. An exception is Piscis Austrinus (the Southern Fish), which contains one bright star, Fomalhaut (see pages 94–95).

PISCES · ARIES · ECLIPTIC · ANDROMEDA · ZENITH · TRIANGULUM · Pleiades · Hyades · M31 · Algol · Aldebaran · PEGASUS · h + χ Per · TAURUS · PERSEUS · ε Aur · δ Cep · CASSIOPEIA · Capella · Betelgeuse · CEPHEUS · AURIGA · ORION · DELPHINUS · Deneb · Polaris · GEMINI · CYGNUS · URSA MAJOR · Castor · SAGITTA · LYRA · URSA MINOR · Pollux · Altair · ε Lyr · CANIS MINOR · Albireo · Vega · DRACO · Dubhe · LYNX · AQUILA

WEST   **NORTH**   **EAST**

A great many constellations go back to the same cycle of myths, though not all the stories are directly related to each other. Thus Cetus, a constellation that reaches its most prominent position high in the southern sky in November, is connected to the Perseus myth, to Pegasus, and to a number of constellations in the northern sky. Cetus was the sea monster that devastated Ethiopia, the land ruled by Cepheus and Cassiopeia (see pages 28–29).

Unlike Perseus and Cassiopeia, **Cetus** (the Whale) has very few bright stars, but one of them, Mira, is of particular interest. (Mira is a Latin word that means wonderful or astounding.) Mira

was the first variable star to be discovered, and it became the prototype of a whole group of variable stars, the Mira-type variables (see pages 150–51). When Mira is at its brightest, it is easy to see with the naked eye; when it is faintest, it can disappear from view.

In the 1960s some astronomers suspected that there might be another wonderful star in Cetus, namely, the star Tau Ceti, which resembles our Sun and is only 12 light-years away. It and Epsilon Eridani were considered the most likely stars to have planets like those of our Sun, planets on which there might be life. American astronomers therefore trained their radio telescopes in the direc-

tions of these two stars and listened intently for signs of some distant civilization, but without success.

North of Cetus stands Pisces, another constellation of the zodiac that is traversed by the ecliptic and where planets therefore could turn up. Pisces, too, is an inconspicuous constellation with few stars visible to the unaided eye. In old sky atlases, this constellation is represented by a pair of fish whose tails are tied together by a rope. According to Greek mythology, Aphrodite, the goddess of love, and her son Eros were fleeing from a raging monster but were unable to cross the Euphrates River in Mesopotamia because of high water. Desperate, they

EAST   SOUTH   WEST

nevertheless plunged into the water, and the sea goddesses took pity on them, sending two fish to their aid. The fish were connected by a rope, which Aphrodite and her son could hold on to. In gratitude for this deed, the gods placed the two fish in the sky. It was in the constellation Pisces that an unusual planetary phenomenon occured in the year 7 B.C., namely, a rare multiple conjunction of Jupiter and Saturn (see page 114). Most modern astronomers now believe that this alignment of the planets in Pisces was the famous star of Bethlehem that announced the birth of Christ. Our present system of counting the years beginning with the birth of Christ—the exact date of which is still the subject of controversy—was not invented until 500 years after the fact.

Cetus

75

ARIES
ZENITH
PISCES
TRIANGULUM
Algol
ANDROMEDA
M31
CASSIOPEIA
Pleiades
PERSEUS
Hyades
TAURUS
Aldebaran
ε Aur
Capella
h + χ Per
AURIGA
ECLIPTIC
GEMINI
Castor
Pollux
δ Cep
PEGASUS
CEPHEUS
CYGNUS
Deneb
Polaris
URSA MINOR
Dubhe
URSA MAJOR
DRACO
CANCER M44
LYNX
HYDRA
LEO

WEST   **NORTH**   **EAST**

In December, the night sky displays the well-known winter constellations during the early evening hours in an advantageous position in the southeast. Unlike in the fall, the south has again clearly become the dominating region of the sky. The ecliptic arches high across the celestial dome, so that during December the planets are in a good viewing position and the Moon is particularly high and keeps shining a long time over the horizon. December is therefore a good time to watch some of the most splendid constellations of the zodiac, especially Gemini, Taurus, and Aries. **Aries** (the Ram) usually is considered the first of the signs of the zodiac. In earlier

times, before the birth of Christ, the Sun was in Aries on the first day of spring, so that that point on the ecliptic, which now usually is referred to as the vernal equinox, was—and sometimes still is—called the first point of Aries. Because of precession, the slow shifting of the celestial sphere's coordinates against the background of the constellations (see pages 104–05), the vernal equinox has meanwhile moved into the constellation Pisces and will in about 400 years reach Aquarius.

The constellation Aries is inseparably linked with the story of Jason and the Argonauts. Their ship, the Argo, accounts for several beautiful constellations in

the southern sky, namely Carina (the Keel), Vela (the Sails), and Puppis (the Stern). One of these, Puppis, can be seen just barely over the southeastern horizon (for more on Argo Navis, see pages 82–83). In Boeotia in ancient Greece there once lived a king by the name of Athamas whose realm was visited by a terrible famine. In desperation, Athamas was ready to sacrifice his two children Phrixus and Hella after the children's wicked stepmother had caused messengers to deliver a false oracle to him. But just before the children were about to be killed, the gods sent a ram with a coat the color of pure gold and with the gift of human speech to save them.

He carried the children aloft and flew eastward with them across the sea. Hella was seized by a sudden panic and lost her hold, plunging down into the water in a spot that to this day is called Hellespont. Phrixus, the boy, was deposited safely in the country of Colchis on the Black Sea. On advice of the gods, Phrixus sacrificed the ram and hung its pelt, the famous golden fleece, in the garden of Ares, the god of war, where a huge dragon guarded it. It was this golden fleece the Argonauts were later commanded by the gods to retrieve, a feat they successfully performed.

Today, Aries is one of the smaller constellations. It has only one relatively bright star, Hamal, which means head of a sheep in Arabic. Hamal is 80 light-years away from us and shines about 70 times brighter than the Sun. The Sun travels past Aries between April 19 and May 13 every year.

Aries

Star Map Series S

This series of star maps is applicable in the countries that lie between the 10th and the 30th degrees of southern latitude. The night sky of the Southern Hemisphere is quite different from that of the Northern Hemisphere. To the observer, the northern constellations seem to be upside down, as a glance at the maps showing the northerly half of the sky immediately demonstrates. The southern constellations even have different kinds of names from those of the north because they go back to much more recent times, namely the eighteenth century. The abbreviations LMC and SMC stand for the two most obvious celestial objects in the southern sky, the Large Magellanic Cloud and the Small Magellanic Cloud. They can be seen in the sky even at full moon as shimmering patches (see page 137).

The farther south one travels in the S-zone, the higher the stars shown in the maps will appear to be above the southern horizon and the lower they will appear to be above the northern horizon. The charts of series S, like those of the two N series, show the sky as it looks at 11 P.M. at the beginning of the month, at 10 P.M. in the middle of the month, and at 9 P.M. at the end of the month.

The star maps S apply to the following countries: Peru, Bolivia, Argentina, Chile, South Africa, Zimbabwe, Tanzania, Botswana, Namibia, Madagascar, and Australia.

What the symbols in the star maps stand for:

◆ = Double stars: Pairs of stars that are particularly close to each other.
◉ = Variable stars: Stars that change in brightness.
□ = Nebulas: Clouds of gas and dust that shine in colors.
∴ = Star clusters: Aggregations of many stars concentrated in one place.
O = Galaxies: Star systems (the Milky Way is one of many galaxies).

About the brightness and size of the stars marked in the maps:

0 = ✹ The brightest stars. They are easily visible even in big city skies.

1 = ●   2 = ●   3 = ●   4 = •   Scale of brightness 0 to 4. The smaller the number, the brighter the star.

This wisplike nebula in the constellation Lyra is probably the remains of a supernova.

January
Star map S 1

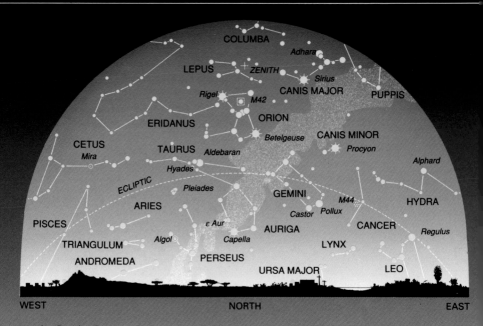

COLUMBA
Adhara
LEPUS ZENITH
Sirius
CANIS MAJOR
PUPPIS
Rigel
M42
ORION
ERIDANUS
Betelgeuse CANIS MINOR
CETUS
Mira
TAURUS Aldebaran
Procyon
Alphard
Hyades
ECLIPTIC
Pleiades
GEMINI
HYDRA
ARIES
Castor Pollux
M44
PISCES
ε Aur
CANCER
Regulus
AURIGA
TRIANGULUM
Algol
Capella
LYNX
ANDROMEDA
PERSEUS
LEO
URSA MAJOR

WEST   **NORTH**   **EAST**

The Sun is closer to Earth in January than at any other time of year. It is only 91 million miles (147.1 million km) away from us. However, the fact that it is now summer in the Southern Hemisphere has little to do with this relative closeness of the Sun, even though the intensity of heat rays does become greater as the distance from their source decreases. But the real reason why there are different seasons of the year is the tilt in Earth's axis (see page 13).

The starry skies of the Southern Hemisphere during the months of January through March are some of the most spectacular anywhere. Seven of the ten brightest stars (all of which are shown in the maps as yellow dots surrounded by small rays) can be seen at an easily viewable height over the horizon. The only ones that are missing are Vega, Arcturus, and Alpha Centauri, though the last mentioned will rise later in the night. The northern part of the sky is dominated by the constellations that include the stars composing what is known in the Northern Hemisphere as the Winter Hexagon. These constellations are Auriga, Taurus, Orion, Canis Major and Canis Minor, and Gemini. In these latitudes and in keeping with the local season, Summer Hexagon would be a more apt term for the Winter Hexagon.

There are many smaller constellations in the southern sky that are named after animals. There are, for instance, **Tucana** (the Toucan), **Phoenix**, **Hydrus** (the Lesser Water Snake), **Volans** (the Flying Fish), **Grus** (the Crane), **Dorado** (the Swordfish), and **Pavo** (the Peacock). These constellations are all grouped around the south celestial pole, which is—in contrast to the north pole—not marked by any bright star but can easily be found with the help of the Southern Cross (see page 22), which is clearly visible at this time of year.

The names of the many exotic animals in the sky of the south do not come from Greek mythology as do the

EAST   SOUTH   WEST

names of constellations in the north, but were invented much later in the seventeenth century. A German astronomer by the name of Johann Bayer, who lived in Augsburg from 1572 to 1625, first presented these constellations to the public in 1603 in his famous star atlas. He used as his sources older reports by Dutch seafarers who had been some of the first Europeans to observe the skies of the Southern Hemisphere in the sixteenth century. Bayer took over various constellations from these accounts, arranging them in rather arbitrary fashion around the south celestial pole, and his draftsmen drew heavily on their imaginations in illustrating them. There is no recognizable resemblance between the star patterns and the animals for which they are named, whereas in the sky of the north the connection between the names and their constellations still can be seen at least to some extent, as in the case of the Ursa Major.

Tucana, Phoenix, Hydrus, Volans, Grus, Dorado, Pavo

WEST   NORTH   EAST

In February, it already is possible to see Centaurus above the horizon in the evening. It, as well as Carina, Vela, and Puppis—parts of Argo Navis—are evidence that some constellations of the southern sky go back to Greek mythology and that not all of them are inventions of the recent past.

Argo Navis (the Ship of the Argonauts) is connected with one of the most exciting adventure stories of Greek mythology. It was originally a single constellation, though today it is split up into four independent parts, which are all adjacent to each other in the sky. A number of other constellations in their vicinity also figure in this famous story.

Jason, the commander of the Argo and its crew, had been sent by his uncle on the dangerous mission of recovering and bringing back to Greece the Golden Fleece. Only after successful completion of this task was he to be allowed to rule over his father's realm. The Golden Fleece was the pelt of the ram that had been sacrificed to the gods after an adventuresome flight across the seas (see pages 76–77). The fleece was in Colchis, fiercely guarded by a dragon.

Jason, aided by Athena, had a big, powerful ship built—the Argo—and advertised throughout Greece the adventure he was setting out on. The most distinguished heroes of the country, in-cluding, among many others, Hercules, Castor, and Pollux (see pages 58–59), responded to the call and joined the Argo's crew. Eventually, of course, Jason succeeded in his mission after killing the dreadful dragon. But before arriving in Colchis, the Argonauts had to pass through many narrow straits where their ship was in great danger of being dashed against the cliffs. However, Athena sent a dove to point the way and guide the Argonauts safely past the rocks, and this dove now stands in the sky, too, near Argo Navis, in the form of the constellation Columba.

The most interesting of the four constellations making up the ship Argo is Carina (the Keel). In it shines

February 1, *11 p.m.*
February 15, 10 p.m.
February 28, 9 p.m.

EAST | SOUTH | WEST

the second brightest star of the heavens, Canopus (see page 133). Another interesting object in this constellation is a large and brilliant star cluster, technically referred to as IC 2602 (this means that it is the 2,602nd entry in the Index Catalogue, a comprehensive listing of star clusters). IC 2602 often is called the southern Pleiades in allusion to the famous Pleiades visible in the sky of the Northern Hemisphere (see pages 147 and 145). It is best to look at IC 2602 through binoculars. Close to the impressive star cluster there is a huge nebula that surrounds the star Eta Carinae. Eta Carinae is an object of the Milky Way, but there is at this point no definite knowledge about its nature (see page 142).

Argo Navis

WEST   NORTH   EAST

In March, the constellations making up Argo Navis dominate the southern sky. **Columba**, which pointed the way through the straits when the Argonauts sailed eastward to retrieve the Golden Fleece, is in the southwest. Above it, Puppis rises up between the two brightest stars of the sky, Sirius and Canopus. Puppis (which means poop or stern in Latin) contains an unusual star, one of the few variables in which one can observe the changes in magnitude with the unaided eye. This is L2 Puppis.

L2 Puppis is a Mira-type variable. Its behavior is similar to that of the wonderful star Mira in Cetus (see pages 140–41). L2 Puppis fluctuates in brightness in a regular cycle of approximately 140 days. At its maximum brightness it is easy to see, but in its dimmest phase its light is at the borderline of what our eyes can detect.

In the southeast, Centaurus and the Southern Cross (Crux) slowly approach their highest point in the sky. The Southern Cross is found in one of the starriest regions of the Milky Way. But within the area of the Southern Cross there is also a particularly dark spot, the so-called Coalsack. There, huge dark clouds of dust block the light of the stars behind them. An especially impressive view of the Coalsack Nebula is obtained through binoculars because one almost has the sense of being in a hole within the band of the Milky Way. The Coalsack Nebula spills into the constellation Musca (the Fly), a rather unusual name first introduced in 1624 by Jakob Bartsch, a son-in-law of Germany's most renowned astronomer Johannes Kepler. The Southern Cross owes its fame primarily to its usefulness as a navigational aid on the seas because its axis points toward the south celestial pole and therefore indicates where south is on the horizon (see pages 22–23). Apart from this, the Southern Cross is not quite as impressive as those in the Northern Hemisphere often imagine. Although the Southern Cross is considered a symbol of Christianity, it already was known to

EAST — SOUTH — WEST

the astronomers of antiquity. But they regarded it as part of Centaurus. Today the Southern Cross holds the record of being the smallest of the 88 constellations in the sky (Hydra is the largest).

In 1942, an exceptionally bright nova appeared in Puppis, a star that blazed to 15 million times its previous brightness within a few days. This amazing outburst of luminosity led astronomers to wonder whether they had witnessed a supernova (see pages 142 and 149), but according to the current state of knowledge this was not the case. At this point all that remains of Nova Puppis 1942 is' an extremely faint star surrounded by some bright, thin clouds of gas that were ejected during the outburst.

Columba

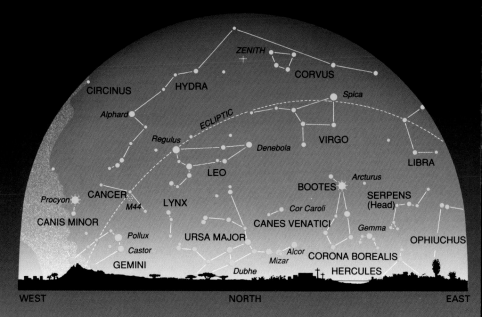

WEST   NORTH   EAST

In April, a glance into the sky straight overhead reveals Hydra in its full, huge length. Hydra is the largest constellation, but it is made up of relatively dim stars (see pages 62–63). Toward the south, **Centaurus** dominates the sky.

Centaurs were fabled beasts from Greek mythology. Half man and half horse, most of them were of gross and violent nature and responsible for much trouble. But there was one exception, the centaur Chiron. He was friendlier and gentler than the rest of his kind, in possession of great wisdom, and a teacher of the art of healing. But his fate took a cruel turn. One day he encountered Hercules, who accidentally dropped one of his poisoned arrows on Chiron's foot. Although Chiron was a master physician, he was unable to heal this wound. His suffering became so unbearable that he wished for death even though he was of divine birth and therefore immortal. By choosing death, he freed Prometheus from his torment.

Centaurus

VIRGO

ZENITH

Spica

CORVUS

ECLIPTIC

Alphard

HYDRA

CENTAURUS

CIRCINUS

LIBRA   ω Cen   VELA   PUPPIS

η Car

CRUX   IC2602

LUPUS   α Cen   MUSCA   VOLANS   L² Pup   CANIS MAJOR

Antares   TRIANGULUM   CARINA   Adhara   Sirius

SCORPIUS   AUSTRALE   OCTANS

OPHIUCHUS   ARA   PAVO   Canopus   COLUMBA

HYDRUS

M7   DORADO   LEPUS   ORION

M8   SAGITTARIUS   SMC   LMC   M42

EAST   SOUTH   WEST

Prometheus had been condemned to eternal suffering because he had stolen fire from the gods and given it to mankind. As a reward for this selfless act, the gods transformed Chiron into the constellation Centaurus.

The constellation Centaurus is famous today primarily for its most brilliant star, Alpha Centauri, one of the ten brightest of the sky. It appears so bright in part because it is closer to our solar system than any other star (see pages 130–31). Centaurus also contains another unusual celestial object, Omega Centauri, the brightest globular star cluster in the sky. The designation Omega (a Greek letter) shows that this star cluster originally

was taken to be a star (see pages 21 and 147), and to the unaided eye it appears to be a star. However, by using a pair of ordinary binoculars one can see its more complex structure, though it appears fuzzy.

Globular clusters are exceptionally compact groupings of huge numbers of stars. This is in contrast to the less dense open star clusters (see page 147), such as IC 2602. The latter appears at this time of year a little farther to the west in Carina. Omega Centauri, which is one of the closest globular star clusters, is about 15,000 light-years away. Intensive observation has shown that Omega Centauri consists of at least 100,000 stars. This does not

mean that all the stars in the cluster are packed closely together. Even in the interior of a globular cluster, individual stars are separated from each other by many billion miles. Still, the celestial view inside a globular star cluster would have to be extraordinary because the sky would be full of stars comparable to Sirius and Canopus and even brighter ones.

CENTAURUS
ZENITH
CORVUS
LIBRA
Spica
HYDRA
Antares
SCORPIUS
VIRGO
SERPENS
(Head)
ECLIPTIC
Denebola
Arcturus
BOOTES
OPHIUCHUS
Gemma
Alphard
Regulus
CANES VENATICI
Cor Caroli
CORONA
LEO
BOREALIS HERCULES
SERPENS
URSA MAJOR
(Tail)
Mizar
DRACO
Alcor
CANCER
M44
LYNX
AQUILA
WEST   NORTH   EAST

Argo Navis with its three constituent constellations Carina, Puppis, and Vela already is quite low in the western sky during this month. Only Vela still reaches up a little higher. West of Vela is the obscure constellation Circinus (the Compass). In spite of its proximity to Argo Navis and the fact that compasses are associated with ships, there is no direct connection between these constellations because at the time when the Argo sailed the seas there was no such thing as a compass.

The name Circinus and that of Octans, the constellation that lies due south, are recent inventions. We owe them to a French astronomer who studied the sky of the Southern Hemisphere intensively from the Cape of Good Hope between 1751 and 1753 and invented the last of the 88 names still used today. This was Nicolas Louis de Lacaille (1713–1762), who made up a total of 14 new constellations. When de Lacaille first watched the southern sky there were only a few constellations in it to look for, namely those that Johann Bayer had created on the basis of descriptions by Dutch navigators (see page 81). De Lacaille was blessed with a lively imagination. He wrote in his catalog of stars: "To fill in the large empty spaces between the old constellations I introduced new ones. The figures I used to represent them are mostly instruments used by practitioners of art and science." Thus he placed in the heavens the Furnace (Fornax), the Clock (Horlogium), the Compass (Circinus), the Octant (Octans), the Microscope (Microscopus), and even an Air Pump (Antlia). These constellations still are recognized today and—compared to the more imaginative names of the northern constellations—give the southern sky a rather prosaic quality, especially since all of de Lacaille's constellations are made up of such dim stars that they can be made out only with great effort. Only two of de Lacaille's 14 constellations have been entered in these maps, namely Circinus and Octans, the latter an instrument for determining altitudes in the sky by using angles of 45 degrees, or an eighth of a full circle (octo is Latin for eight). Better known than Octans is **Sextans**, which was named by Hevelius. The sextant, an instrument similar to the octant, uses 60-degree angles (a sixth of a full circle).

Neither Circinus nor Sextans is remarkable for anything in particular, and Octans, too, displays only a few faint stars. Its claim to fame rests on the fact that the south celestial pole falls within its confines. However, Octans is of no use when trying to find the south celestial pole quickly. For this purpose, one turns to the Southern Cross and extends the line of its axis by four times its length (see page 22).

In the northern part of the sky, Arcturus is the most prominent spot of light during May. Together with Spica in Virgo and Regulus in Leo, it forms the Vernal Triangle. In the Southern Hemisphere it would, of course, be more logical to call it the Autumnal Triangle.

Sextans

WEST   NORTH   EAST

At the beginning of winter in the Southern Hemisphere, the ecliptic rises up steeply and passes through the zenith. This means that the planets that are visible in June are in an exceptionally favorable position, almost directly overhead.

The dominant constellations in the south are now Centaurus, the Southern Cross, and—almost at the zenith—Scorpius and Sagittarius. The Milky Way runs through all these constellations, presenting an impressive aspect in June. The most conspicuous objects in the Milky Way, the globular star cluster Omega Centauri and the open star cluster IC 2602 in Carina, as well as the gigantic nebula M 8 in Sagittarius and the variable star Eta Carinae are all in positions where they can be seen clearly through binoculars. Altogether, the southern part of the sky is filled in June with a variety of objects that invite closer inspection. In addition there are **Triangulum Australe**, (the Southern Triangle) and **Pavo**, (the Peacock), constellations first described in 1603 by the German astronomer Johann Bayer, who based his work on accounts of early seafarers.

There is a rather interesting story concerning the Southern Triangle. According to it the Dutch writer Peter Caesius suggested in the seventeenth century naming these three stars after the Old Testament patriarchs Abraham, Isaac, and Jacob. The stars forming the Southern Triangle therefore also are known as the Patriarch Stars. As this story shows, the constellations have not always been as immutably defined and named as they are today. There were not only many attempts to create new constellations, as Johann Bayer did in the case of Triangulum Australe and Pavo, and, later, Johannes Hevelius—not to mention the Frenchman de Lacaille and his scientific instruments—but also suggestions to abolish or rename old ones.

In the seventeenth century, there was a movement to replace old constellation names that were deemed heathen with Christian ones.

EAST   SOUTH   WEST

The 12 constellations of the Zodiac, for instance, were to be called after the twelve apostles. In 1627, the German astronomer Julius Schiller published a work called *The Christian Night Sky*. According to this book, Argo Navis, whose sails (Vela) are the last part of the ship to sink below the horizon during the early evening hours in June, was to be turned into Noah's Ark. Further, Schiller fashioned the archangel St. Raphael out of the constellations Tucana and Hydrus and the Small Magellanic Cloud. Lyra, which appears in June, became Christ's manger. However, Schiller's attempt to Christianize the starry sky did not prove very successful.

Ara (the Altar) is one of the most southerly constellations that were known in the ancient world. It can just barely be seen from the Mediterranean region. Ara was said to have been the place where the Olympian gods formed an alliance to defeat the Titans. In commemoration of their victory, the gods placed the altar in the heavens.

Triangulum Australe and Pavo

91

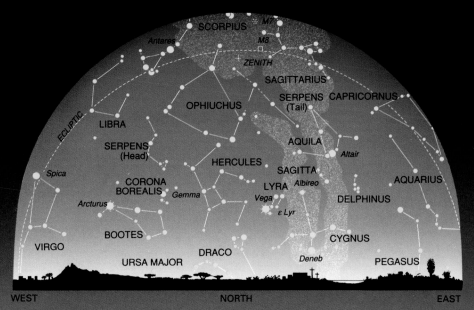

SCORPIUS M7
Antares M8
ZENITH
SAGITTARIUS
SERPENS CAPRICORNUS
OPHIUCHUS (Tail)
LIBRA
SERPENS AQUILA
(Head) Altair
HERCULES
Spica SAGITTA
CORONA LYRA Albireo
BOREALIS Gemma Vega
Arcturus DELPHINUS
ε Lyr
BOOTES AQUARIUS
VIRGO CYGNUS
DRACO
URSA MAJOR Deneb PEGASUS

WEST **NORTH** **EAST**

Starting in July, the view into the sky directly over-head is particularly reward-ing. The ecliptic runs through the zenith, where there are also two famous constella-tions of the zodiac with a number of unusual celestial objects. They are Scorpius and, of special interest, **Sag-ittarius** (the Archer). Push-ing between these two con-stellations and also within the belt of the zodiac, is Ophiu-chus, which does not, how-ever, add any bright stars to the ecliptic the way Scorpius does. As part of the redrawing of all the constellations' boundaries in 1930, Ophiu-chus was assigned a space between Scorpius and Sagit-tarius and thus became the thirteenth constellation in the zodiac.

Sagittarius is one of the most interesting constella-tions of the zodiac, for it lies against the center of the Milky Way. July is a particularly good time to observe the Milky Way anyway because its faintly luminous band also crosses the zenith—as does the ecliptic—rising from Cygnus in the northeast, passing through Sagittarius and Scorpius, and descend-ing down to Carina in the southwest. The Milky Way is a vast star system or gal-axy, 100,000 light-years in diameter, on the outer regions of which Earth and our Sun are located (see page 140). The center of the galaxy is about 28,000 light-years away from our solar system,

but it cannot be seen because the view is blocked by too many stars as well as by gas and dust nebulas.

Consequently it is not known at this point exactly what lies hidden in the center of the Milky Way. It is pos-sible that some explosion-like processes took place there that produced huge masses of gases. This theory has been deduced in part from the analysis of radio waves that, unlike visible light, can pen-etrate directly to us from the center of the galaxy. Astron-omers estimate that the core of the Milky Way contains a mass equivalent to that of 500 million suns.

Sagittarius, in which lie a number of the most beautiful celestial objects—the gas

EAST   SOUTH   WEST

nebula M 8 (see page 142) and the star cluster M 7 (see pages 148 and 21), for example—is one of the classical constellations of the zodiac. Sagittarius usually is depicted in the shape of a centaur—a half human, half horse. In this respect it resembles Centaurus, which is still fully visible in July in the southwestern sky.

The stories associated with Sagittarius, centering around the wise centaur Chiron, are the same ones that are told in connection with the constellation Centaurus (see pages 86–87). The Chinese, on the other hand, saw a tiger, which is a figure of their zodiac, in place of Sagittarius, and Julius Schiller, in his abortive attempt to Christianize the starry sky, replaced Sagittarius with the apostle Matthew. Two thousand years before our era, the Babylonians saw in the constellation we call Sagittarius the King of War, Nergal, which they represented in the shape of a centaur. The conception of Sagittarius as a fabled creature therefore must be of great antiquity.

Sagittarius

WEST   NORTH   EAST

August is the month of the Perseids, a famous meteor shower (see page 139). Between August 10 and 12 a large number of meteors or shooting stars seem to emanate from the constellation Perseus. Unfortunately Perseus is not visible in August in the early evening. It doesn't rise until about 2 A.M, when it appears in the northeast (see table, page 20).

The Milky Way still presents a glorious view in the southern part of the sky. Sagittarius and Scorpius, where the Milky Way shows its greatest variety, are still almost directly overhead. In the southeast, Achernar, the brightest star in the constellation Eridanus, is again plainly visible. Above it, one can spot two other constellations that appear quite prominent because they are in an otherwise starless area of the sky. They are **Piscis Austrinus** (the Southern Fish) and **Grus** (the Crane).

The Crane, named by Dutch sailors, is one of the animal constellations first described in 1603 by Johann Bayer. Piscis Austrinus, on the other hand, has been known as a constellation since ancient times, but its origin is no longer very clear. In older representations, as in Hevelius's star atlas, the Southern Fish usually is shown with its mouth wide open, drinking the water poured into it by neighboring Aquarius. Fomalhaut, whose name means the fish's mouth, is the brightest star in Piscis Austrinus and, in fact, in a large area of the surrounding sky. It is not a particularly large star and is separated from our solar system by only 22 light-years. It is estimated to be about twice the size of our Sun and about 14 times as luminous. In 1983, a satellite launched above Earth's atmosphere to conduct an infrared search of the sky detected a dust nebula around Fomalhaut. This discovery suggests that a planetary system similar to our own may be in the process of forming around Fomalhaut. On such planets that orbit around and derive their energy from a star, conditions might exist that could give rise to some kind of life

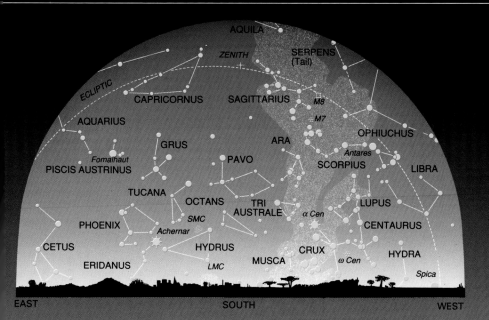

forms. Fomalhaut, together with a star in Eridanus (see pages 98–99) and another one in Cetus (see pages 74–75) are therefore among the star systems in which life might conceivably exist. However, at this point in time we have no sign indicating that this is the case. An expedition to Fomalhaut—or to other stars that may be forming planets—is out of the question. Even if we had space vehicles that traveled at speeds approaching that of light, the journey would take 22 years.

The constellation Grus has little of special interest to offer. But its stars are relatively bright, so that this constellation is easy to pick out in this otherwise starless region of the sky. The area around Grus thus presents a clear contrast to the sky around Sagittarius and Scorpius, through which runs one of the brightest sections of the Milky Way.

Piscis Austrinus and Grus

95

September, which ushers in autumn in the Northern Hemisphere and marks the beginning of spring on the southern half of Earth, is also the month of the New Year for many cultures. Many calendars other than the one we go by begin the new year at the onset of fall or spring. The Jewish and the Persian calendars are examples.

By September the brightest stars in the southern part of the sky have moved on and in the north the brightest ones have not yet returned. Unlike in January or March, very few of the brightest stars of the southern sky are visible. They are Alpha Centauri, which can be seen shortly before it sets in the southwest, Achernar in the southeast, and Vega in the north. A constellation that is not among the most spectacular but has an interesting history, now can be seen low in the southwest. It is **Lupus** (the Wolf).

The name Lupus is of relatively recent origin. Among the Greeks and Romans, this constellation was an unspecified wild animal. Perhaps it was the wolf—or rather she-wolf—that saved Romulus and Remus, the founders of the city of Rome from dying of hunger after they had been abandoned as babies in the forest. This wolf later became an important symbol of the Roman Empire. When an attempt was made much later to bring the sky under the sphere of influence of the Christian faith, Lupus became Benjamin, the ancestor of one of the 12 tribes of Israel.

Almost 1,000 years ago, in the year 1006, Lupus was the site of one of the biggest supernovas ever to be observed. Many who witnessed it in Arabia and in China were so struck by the event that they left precise descriptions. The Arabian astronomer Ali ibn Ridwan of Cairo, for instance, wrote: "At the beginning of my education I witnessed a unique spectacle. A huge star appeared in Scorpius, in the opposite direction of the Sun. This star was round in shape and about two or three times the size of Venus. It lit up the horizon, and its light flickered strongly. It

AQUARIUS

ZENITH

CAPRICORNUS

ECLIPTIC

Fomalhaut

PISCIS AUSTRINUS

GRUS

AQUILA

SERPENS
(Tail)

SAGITTARIUS

CETUS

M8

PHOENIX

PAVO

ARA

M7

TUCANA

SCORPIUS

Achernar

SMC

OPHIUCHUS

ERIDANUS

Antares

HYDRUS

TRIANGULUM
AUSTRALE

OCTANS

α Cen

LMC

CENTAURUS

LUPUS

LIBRA

DORADO

MUSCA

EAST

SOUTH

WEST

was more than a quarter of the Moon's brightness."

Supernovas are the most spectacular events involving fixed stars. What happens is that a star explodes suddenly and unexpectedly, throwing off into space most of its matter, a process that briefly releases unimaginably vast quantities of energy. In the course of recorded history, only very few supernova explosions visible to the naked eye have been observed. The most recent one took place in 1987 in the Large Magellanic Cloud (see page 137). The last supernova to have been seen in our galaxy occurred in 1604 in the constellation Ophiuchus (see pages 66–67).

Astronomers have been trying for a long time to track down remains of the supernova of 1006 in the constellation Lupus, but so far no conclusive evidence has been found because the position given in the old reports is too imprecise.

Lupus

October
Star map S 10

WEST | NORTH | EAST

The constellation Eridanus (the River) first can be seen in its full length in the southeastern sky in October. It is not the largest constellation of the sky (this rank belongs to Hydra), but it is, along with Hydra, among the longest that can be clearly traced at this time of year. **Eridanus** starts low in the sky, next to Rigel in Orion, and meanders upward in many curves, ending with the star Achernar, one of the brightest stars in the sky (see page 130).

In Greek mythology, Eridanus was the river into which Phaeton, the son of the sun god, plunged after his wild journey across the sky. Phaeton had asked his father, Helios, to let him drive the

sun chariot, but Helios, worried about his son's safety, asked him to give up this wish. Phaeton, however, was determined to have his way and paid no heed to his

father's warnings. The horses yanked the chariot around furiously as Phaeton was trying to steer them through the constellations of the zodiac. He became frightened and

Eridanus

98

EAST   SOUTH   WEST

lost control of the horses. According to some accounts, the chariot's mad careening across the sky created the Milky Way (see also page 140). In any case, the fiery chariot came so close to Earth that it scorched the people of Ethiopia, leaving them black, and turned Libya into a red-hot desert. Eventually Phaeton was hurled into the river Eridanus, where the nymphs that lived there recovered and buried his body. The gods raised Eridanus to the heavens but not Phaeton.

Eridanus contains another star, apart from Achernar, which, though not especially conspicuous, frequently is mentioned when the question comes up whether there might

be life on some planet in outer space. It is Epsilon Eridani, which bears a very close resemblance to our Sun. It is of about the same size and brightness and is a relatively close neighbor, a mere 11 light-years away. Because of these similarities, some people have suspected that Epsilon Eridani might have a planetary system similar to that of our Sun and that life might have evolved there as it did on Earth. That is why a project was initiated in 1960 of examining Epsilon Eridani and another look-alike of the Sun in Cetus intensively through a radio telescope, scanning them at a wavelength of 21 cm. The hope was that signals from an extraterrestrial civilization

might be detected. The result was negative. To date, not a single signal has been received from Epsilon Eridani that gives any indication of artificial origin and might thus have been sent by creatures on a distant planet.

Next to Achernar is Phoenix, another constellation that was first introduced by Johann Bayer in 1603.

99

ZENITH

Fomalhaut

PISC
AUSTR

CETUS

Mira

ERIDANUS

AQUARIUS

LEPUS

CAPRICORNUS

PISCES

ECLIPTIC

Rigel

ARIES

TAURUS

M42

TRIANGULUM

Hyades

ORION

Pleiades

Aldebaran

PERSEUS

PEGASUS

M31

ANDROMEDA

Algol

Betelgeuse

DELPHINUS

CASSIOPEIA

h + χ Per

ε Aur

GEMINI

CYGNUS

δ Cep

Capella

AURIGA

AQUILA

WEST   NORTH   EAST

In the eastern sky, Orion is now particularly prominent. For stargazers in the Northern Hemisphere, this constellation has an unusual look because Orion seems to be standing on its head. Sirius, the brightest star of all, along with Canopus, is again in a good viewing position in the eastern sky, too. Sirius, Canopus, and Achernar stand in a more or less straight line and are of aid in getting oriented in the sky, especially at dusk, when not many other stars are yet visible.

Between Sirius and Orion a constellation with the unusual name Lepus (the Hare) shows up in the southeastern sky. This, too, is a classical constellation that already was

known to the ancient civilizations. Its exact origin is unclear. Because its position is south of Orion, it might have represented some game animal that the heavenly hunter Orion was chasing.

Also in a good position for easy viewing are Tucana (the Toucan) and **Capricornus** (the Sea Goat). The latter is one of the constellations of the classical zodiac (see page 16), whereas the former is one of the constellations introduced by Johann Bayer. Although not particularly impressive otherwise, Tucana includes one of the notable objects in the southern sky, the Small Magellanic Cloud, which—along with the Large Magellanic Cloud in Dorado—is among the

most striking celestial objects in the sky of the Southern Hemisphere.

The earliest modern mention of the Small Magellanic Cloud (see page 137) and of its larger namesake goes back to the first journey around the world in 1520, headed by Ferdinand Magellan. The clouds are named for the explorer, even though he was killed in the Philippines and his crew had to complete the journey without their leader. The Large and the Small Magellanic Clouds are the galaxies that lie closest to our solar system. They are irregular galaxies, that is, they have no particular shape. The Small Magellanic Cloud is somewhat farther away from us than the Large one. These two galaxies are the prime objects of observation on which the telescopes located in the Southern Hemisphere are trained. Both galaxies are so close to the south celestial pole that they are never visible in the mid-latitudes of the north. Until about the 1950s the stars of the northern sky were studied much more thoroughly than those seen only in the Southern Hemisphere. This has changed dramatically within the last 30 years, as many observatories in the Northern Hemisphere, especially those in the United States and in Europe, have set up associate institutions on the southern continents. Thus, eight European nations have established the European Southern Observatory (ESO), which now maintains a huge observatory on La Sillia, a mountaintop in Chile.

November, finally, is the month of the Leonids, a large meteor shower. In the middle of the month, exceptionally large numbers of meteors appear to burst forth from within the constellation Leo (see page 60).

Capricornus

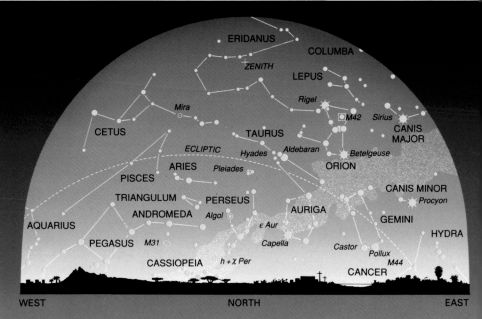

ERIDANUS
COLUMBA
ZENITH
LEPUS
Rigel
Mira
M42 Sirius
CETUS
TAURUS
CANIS MAJOR
ECLIPTIC Hyades Aldebaran
Betelgeuse
ARIES Pleiades
PISCES
ORION
CANIS MINOR
TRIANGULUM PERSEUS
Procyon
ANDROMEDA Algol
AURIGA
ε Aur
GEMINI
AQUARIUS
Capella
PEGASUS M31
Castor
HYDRA
CASSIOPEIA h + χ Per
Pollux
M44
CANCER

WEST　　　　　　　　NORTH　　　　　　　　EAST

In studying the star maps for the month of December, one soon is struck by the fact that among the various types of names for constellations there is one group of animals that is unusually well represented, namely fish. In addition to Pisces, one of the constellations of the classical zodiac, we find Cetus (the Whale), Volans (the Flying Fish), Piscis Austrinus (the Southern Fish), and, finally, Dorado (the Swordfish). The last of these, Dorado, was invented and placed in the sky rather arbitrarily by Johann Bayer in 1603 and hardly would be worth special mention if it were not the site of the most glamorous object of the southern sky, the Large Ma-gellanic Cloud. Even on nights when the full moon is out, the Large Magellanic Cloud can be seen plainly with the naked eye as a large, fuzzy patch of light, which, when viewed through binoculars or—to even more dramatic effect—through a telescope, reveals itself as a huge accumulation of innumerable stars.

Triangulum

The Large Magellanic Cloud—named, like its smaller counterpart, for the explorer-navigator Magellan—is the galaxy that lies closest to Earth. It is only about 150,000 light-years distant, and astronomers estimate that it contains between 15 and 30 million stars. The Large Magellanic Cloud includes a number of nebulas, star clusters, and other objects, all of which stand out in beautiful colors in photographs of the cloud (see pages 152–53).

The Large Magellanic Cloud gained further fame in 1987, when a supernova was discovered there. This supernova, which technically is referred to as 1987 A, is the most recent supernova that could be seen by the unaided eye (see page 149). This supernova is particularly interesting because it was the first time that such an event could be recorded by the entire array of technological instruments at the disposal of modern astronomy. It therefore was observed by satellites as well as by all available telescopes on the southern half of the globe. An unusual signal originating in this distant astral explosion was recorded even in the deep shafts of mines, where the impact of neutrinos could be registered.

In the northern part of the sky there is a third distant galaxy that also is visible to the unaided eye. It is the Andromeda Galaxy, technically known as M 31. South of it lies the small constellation **Triangulum** (the Triangle), one of the few that goes back to ancient times and is named after an object rather than a mythological figure. In this case there is even a close resemblance between the object and its representation in the sky. Above Triangulum the ecliptic cuts across the sky in a low arc in December. The planets and the Moon, which travel along the ecliptic, are therefore also relatively low in the northern sky.

Celestial Events up to the Year 2000

The stars and the constellations formed by them always appear in the same place in the sky every year at the same time. They rise and set, thus demonstrating Earth's rotation around its own axis (see The Movement of Earth on page 8). The mind-boggling, truly astronomical distances that separate them from Earth prevent us from perceiving their own motion—the so-called proper motion—at which they travel through space. Only heavenly bodies that are much closer to us than the stars display motion that can be discerned clearly from Earth as these bodies wander from one constellation to the next, continually changing position in relation to each other and to the stars that shine behind them. There are only a few of these movable heavenly bodies that are visible to the naked eye. But they constitute the most striking and spectacular celestial sights. Important events of this kind include the Sun in its relation to Earth; the Moon; eclipses resulting from the interplay of the Sun, the Moon, and Earth; and the major planets Mercury, Venus, Mars, Jupiter, and Saturn.

Unfortunately there is no way to predict the equally if not even more spectacular appearances of comets or shooting stars and of supernovas, the sudden, dramatic blazing up of stars (see pages 133 and 149). To keep abreast of these events, all you can do is follqw reports in the daily press.

Predictable Facts Concerning the Sun, Earth, and the Beginning of the Seasons

Earth and the Sun are one inseparable unit in space. Without the Sun there could be no life on Earth, for only the Sun's energy, which has been radiating over Earth for more than five billion years, makes life possible here (concerning the Sun, see page 149).

The rising and setting of the Sun determines the rhythm of our days, and ever since man first appeared on Earth, the day has been the natural unit by which he has measured time. Earth's orbit around the Sun defines the length of the year, which is equivalent to 365¼ revolutions of Earth around its axis. The motions of Earth and the Sun consequently form the basis of our calendar. Depending on the geographic latitude, the Sun rises and sets at different hours in the course of the year (see page 12), and depending on the season it is higher or lower in the sky and thus determines the length of the day (see pages 12–13).

The Beginning of the Seasons

Northern Hemisphere Southern Hemisphere	Spring Fall		Summer Winter		Fall Spring		Winter Summer	
1992	3/20	3:48 AM	6/20	10:14 AM	9/22	1:43 PM	12/21	9:43 PM
1993	3/20	9:40 AM	6/21	4:00 AM	9/22	7:22 PM	12/21	3:26 PM
1994	3/20	3:28 PM	6/21	9:47 AM	9/23	1:19 AM	12/21	9:23 PM
1995	3/20	9:14 PM	6/21	3:34 PM	9/23	7:13 PM	12/22	3:17 AM
1996	3/20	3:03 AM	6/20	9:24 PM	9/22	1:00 PM	12/21	9:06 AM
1997	3/20	8:55 AM	6/21	3:20 AM	9/22	6:56 PM	12/21	3:07 PM
1998	3/20	2:55 PM	6/21	9:02 AM	9/23	12:37 AM	12/21	8:57 PM
1999	3/20	8:46 PM	6/21	2:49 PM	9/23	6:32 AM	12/22	2:44 AM
2000	3/20	2:35 AM	6/20	8:48 PM	9/22	12:28 PM	12/21	8:38 AM

Because of leap year, the dates marking the beginning of the seasons change in a four-year cycle.

The table on page 104 shows the exact time when spring, summer, fall, and winter begin in the years 1992 to 2000. In the Northern Hemisphere, the Sun is highest in the sky and shines the longest at the beginning of summer. After that it seems to sink lower and lower until it crosses to the south side of the celestial equator at the beginning of fall, at the so-called autumnal equinox. Three months later, at the onset of winter in the north and of summer in the south, the Sun reaches its lowest point in the sky of the Northern Hemisphere and the highest point in the sky of the southern half of the globe. This time is called a solstice because the sun "comes to a stop." It sinks no lower but starts rising higher again until, when it is spring in the Northern Hemisphere (fall on the southern half of the globe), it recrosses the equator, this time moving from south to north. This point of the year is called the vernal equinox, because once again—as at the autumnal equinox—day and night are almost exactly the same length.

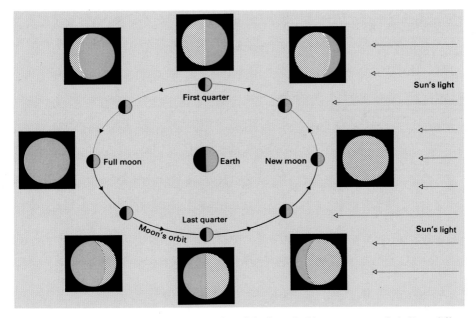

Depending on its position in relation to Earth and the Sun, the Moon, as we see it, is lit up differently by the Sun's light. The pictures in the black squares show how it appears to us in the sky.

All Phases of the Moon Can Be Predicted Accurately

The Moon is the heavenly body nearest to us—Earth's companion on the journey through space. It orbits continually around Earth and, along with Earth, travels around the Sun. The Moon is the only celestial body (apart from the Sun) that appears as a disk to the naked eye and on whose surface one clearly can see lighter and darker areas.

As it circles around Earth, the Moon is illuminated by the Sun—just like Earth—

and keeps changing in appearance, passing through the different lunar phases we all know. The diagram on page 105 shows how these phases come about. The whole cycle of the Moon's phases—the transformation from invisible new moon to a crescent in the evening sky that waxes gradually fatter night after night until half of the Moon's face is lit up at what is called the first quarter; the continued growth into a round disk when the Moon is full and stays in the sky all night; then the waning to the "last quarter," when the Moon shines only during the second half of the night; and, finally, the return to new moon—takes about 29½ days. This cycle and the time it takes to complete it is the basis of a further unit of measuring time, the lunar, or synodic, month. In many ancient cultures, the lunar month was a more important time unit than the year. In old myths it often determined the course of events, and in many ancient calendar systems the months corresponded exactly to the actual lunar phases. In our modern calendar, the months are merely divisions of the year and bear no relationship to the actual phases of the Moon.

But even today the changes of the lunar phases are one of the most prominent processes taking place in the sky, and all the special points of the lunar cycle—the dates of the two half moons, the full moon, and the new moon—are listed in the following table for the years 1992 to 2000.

Note: Lunar eclipses only occur during the full moon; solar eclipses occur only during the new moon.

Lunar Phases 1992–2000

	JAN	FEB	MAR	APR	MAY	JUN	JUL	AUG	SEP	OCT	NOV	DEC
1992	4●	3●	4●	2●	2●	7◑	6◑	5◑	3◑	3◑	2◑	2◑
	12◐	11◐	11◐	10◐	9◐	14○	14○	13○	11○	11○	10○	9○
	19○	18○	18○	16○	16○	23◑	22◑	21◑	19◑	18◑	17◑	16◑
	26◑	25◑	25◑	24◑	24◑	30●	29●	27●	26●	25●	24●	23●
					31●							31◐
1993	8○	6○	1◐	6○	5○	4○	3○	2○	9◑	8◑	7◑	6◑
	14◑	13◑	8○	13◑	13◑	12◑	11◑	10◑	15●	15●	13●	13●
	22●	21●	14◑	21●	21●	19●	19●	17●	22◐	22◐	20◐	20◐
	30◐		23●	29◐	28◐	26◐	25◐	24◐	30○	30○	29○	28○
			30◐				31○					
1994	4◑	3◑	4◑	2◑	2◑	9●	8●	7●	5●	4●	3●	2●
	11●	10●	12●	10●	10●	16◐	15◐	14◐	12◐	11◐	10◐	9◐
	19◐	18◐	20◐	18◐	18◐	23○	22○	21○	19○	19○	18○	17○
	27○	25○	27○	25○	24○	30◑	30◑	29◑	27◑	27◑	26◑	25◑
					31◑							

Lunar Phases 1992-2000

Year	JAN	FEB	MAR	APR	MAY	JUN	JUL	AUG	SEP	OCT	NOV	DEC
1995	1●	7◐	1●	8◐	7◐	6◐	5◐	3◐	2◐	1◐	7○	6○
	8◐	15○	9◐	**15○**	14○	12○	12○	10○	8○	8○	15◑	15◑
	16○	22◑	16○	21◑	21◑	19◑	19◑	17◑	16◑	16◑	22●	21●
	23◑		23◑	**29●**	29●	27●	27●	25●	24●	**24●**	29◐	28◐
	30●		30●							30◐		
1996	5○	4○	5○	3○	3○	1○	7◑	5◑	4◑	4◑	3◑	3◑
	13◑	12◑	12◑	10◑	9◑	8◑	15●	14●	13●	**12●**	10●	10●
	20●	19●	19●	**17●**	17●	15●	23◐	21◐	20◐	19◐	17◐	17◐
	27◐	26◐	26◐	25◐	25◐	24◐	30○	28○	**26○**	26○	24○	24○
						30○						
1997	1◑	7●	2◑	7●	6●	5●	4●	3●	1●	1●	7◐	7◐
	8●	14◐	**8●**	14◐	14◐	12◐	12◐	11◐	9◐	9◐	14○	13○
	15◐	22○	15◐	22○	22○	19○	19○	18○	**16○**	15○	21◑	21◑
	23○		**23○**	29◑	29◑	27◑	26◑	24◑	23◑	22◑	29●	29●
	31◑		31◑							31●		
1998	5◐	3◐	5◐	3◐	3◐	1◐	1◐	7○	6○	5○	4○	3○
	12○	11○	12○	11○	11○	10○	9○	14◑	12◑	12◑	10◑	10◑
	20◑	19◑	21◑	19◑	18◑	17◑	16◑	**21●**	20●	20●	18●	18●
	28●	**26●**	27●	26●	25●	23●	23●	30◐	28◐	28◐	26◐	26◐
							31◐					
1999	1○	8◑	2○	8◑	8◑	7◑	6◑	4◑	2◑	2◑	7●	7●
	9◑	**16●**	10◑	15●	15●	13●	12●	**11●**	9●	9●	16◐	15◐
	17●	22◐	17●	22◐	22◐	20◐	20◐	18◐	17◐	17◐	23○	22○
	24◐		24◐	30○	30○	28○	**28○**	26○	25○	24○	29◑	29◑
	31○		31○							31◑		
2000	6●	**5●**	6●	4●	3●	2●	**1●**	6◐	5◐	5◐	4◐	3◐
	14◐	12◐	13◐	11◐	10◐	8◐	8◐	15○	13○	13○	11○	11○
	20○	19○	19○	18○	18○	16○	**16○**	22◑	20◑	20◑	18◑	17◑
	28◑	26◑	27◑	26◑	26◑	24◑	24◑	29●	27●	27●	25●	**25●**
							30●					

Numbers printed in boldface indicate lunar eclipses if next to ○ and solar eclipses if next to ●

● *New moon*   ◐ *First quarter waxing half moon*   ○ *Full moon*   ◑ *Last quarter waning half moon*

Dates, Duration, and Visibility of Solar Eclipses

The Moon's circling around Earth is responsible for what are probably the most dramatic celestial events: the solar and lunar eclipses. A solar eclipse occurs when the Moon stands between Earth and the Sun, blocking the sunlight and casting its shadow across Earth.

A lunar eclipse occurs when Earth stands between the Sun and the Moon and casts its shadow across the surface of the Moon (see diagram below).

From these two statements an important law can be deduced, namely, that solar eclipses can occur only during new moon (the only time when the Moon stands between Earth and the Sun) and lunar eclipses can occur only during full moon (the only time when the Moon is at the exact opposite point of the sky from the Sun, with Earth on the line between them). You can see very clearly that this law holds if you look at the table of the lunar phases on pages 106 and 107, where the solar and lunar eclipses for the years 1991 to 2000 are entered. (The exact dates are printed in boldface.)

Both the shadow of the Moon and the shadow of Earth are made up of two parts. Because both bodies are spherical, they cast conical shadows that consist of an outer and an inner cone. The inner cone points away from the Sun (or Earth), whereas the outer cone points toward the Sun (or Earth). The resulting shadows are called, respectively, the umbra and the penumbra. The interplay between them results in different kinds of eclipses. The umbra of the Moon is almost exactly the same length as the mean distance between Earth and the Moon, that is,

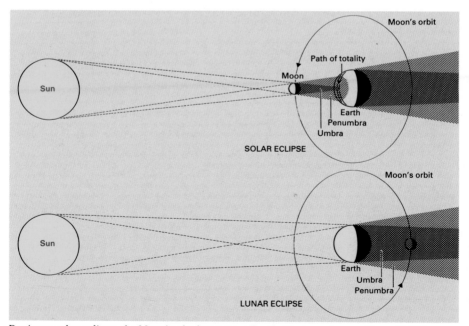

During a solar eclipse, the Moon's shadow covers Earth. During a lunar eclipse, Earth's shadow covers the Moon.

approximately 240,000 miles (380,000 km). Consequently the tip of the umbra just barely reaches the surface of Earth, where it covers an area of maximally 170 miles (273 km) in diameter. Around this area there is a considerably larger circle (up to 4,400 miles or 7,000 km across!) that is reached by the penumbra. In the umbral area the Sun appears completely covered (see photo, page 110), whereas in the area of the penumbra it is only partially covered (see photos on this page).

While the Moon's shadow falls on Earth's surface, both Earth and the Moon continue to move, Earth rotating around its axis from west to east, and the Moon traveling along in the same direction. The result of this motion is that the umbra as well as the penumbra flit across Earth's surface at great speed (about 1,500 miles or 2,400 km per hour!), always from west to east. (The exact paths they take across the globe's surface are indicated on the maps of the most important solar eclipses reproduced on the flap and the inside front cover.)

The dates of all eclipses through the year 2000 are listed in the table on pages 110 and 111. Included there are two other kinds of solar eclipses: partial eclipses and annular eclipses. If the Moon is too far north or south of the Sun at new moon, only the penumbra may reach Earth's surface, resulting in a partial solar eclipse. Such eclipses are visible only in the extreme northern and southern latitudes, that is in the Arctic and nearby regions and on Antarctica. During an annular eclipse, the Moon's umbra hits the surface of Earth, just as during a total eclipse. But because the distances between Earth and the Sun and between Earth and the Moon fluctuate, it sometimes happens that the Moon's umbra doesn't quite reach Earth's surface. If one then stands on a point that is directly in line with the umbra's tip, one witnesses the strange sight of the Moon's disk blocking the Sun but not covering it

A rare celestial event: The partially eclipsed Sun drops below the horizon on July 20, 1982, as seen in Hamburg, Germany.

completely, as it would during a total eclipse. Instead, a narrow ring of the Sun's surface still shows around the dark moon. That is why this kind of eclipse is called annular (from Latin *annulus*, ring).

Total and annular solar eclipses (less so the partial ones) surely constitute the most dramatic celestial phenomena of all. It is only during a total solar eclipse that the solar corona in its full extent can be seen. The corona (a garland or crown of light surrounding the Sun) is the Sun's atmosphere, which consists of hot, highly dissipated gases (see page 149) and extends several million miles into space. It appears in ever changing forms from one eclipse to another and offers a spectacular scene. The sudden darkness that falls over Earth in the middle of the day, the emergence of the brighter stars in the sky, and the reactions of natural creatures and organisms for whom this sudden darkness comes as a complete surprise—all this turns a total solar eclipse into an unforgettable experience.

Because the Moon's umbra narrows down to such a small area by the time it reaches Earth's surface, total solar eclipses are extremely rare in any one particular country. Partial solar eclipses are considerably more

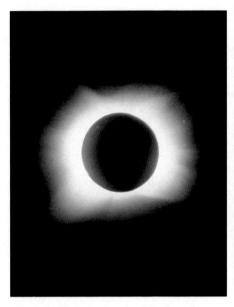

When the Moon covers the Sun, the solar corona becomes visible (Java, June 11, 1983).

common because the Moon's penumbra measures about 4,400 miles (7,000 km) in diameter, compared to a maximum of 170 miles (273 km) for the umbra.

Solar Eclipses: When and Where They Are Visible

Date	Type	Peak of Eclipse	Duration of Peak Obscurity	Maximum Extent of Solar Disk Obscured
Jan. 15, 1991	a	6:53 P.M.	7 min, 53 sec	93%
Visibility: Tasmania, New Zealand; partial in Australia, Oceania, Pacific, Antarctica				
July 11, 1991	t	2:06 P.M.	6 min, 54 sec	108%
Visibility: See front of book				
Jan. 4, 1992	a	6:05 P.M.	11 min, 41 sec	92%
Visibility: Pacific; partial in northern Australia, Oceania, New Guinea				
June 30, 1992	t	7:10 A.M.	5 min, 21 sec	106%
Visibility: Southern Atlantic; partial in South America, West and South Africa				
Dec. 23, 1992	p	7:31 P.M.	—	84%
Visibility: Japan, Korea, northern Pacific				
May 21, 1993	p	9:19 A.M.	—	74%
Visibility: Canada, USA, Greenland, northern Europe, northern USSR				

Solar Eclipses 1991–2000

Solar Eclipses: When and Where They Are Visible

Date	Type	Peak of Eclipse	Duration of Peak Obscurity	Maximum Extent of Solar Disk Obscured
Nov. 13, 1993	p	4:45 P.M.	—	93%
Visibility: Antarctica, New Zealand				
May 10, 1994	a	12:11 P.M.	6 min, 14 sec	94%
Visibility: See front of book				
Nov. 3, 1994	t	7:39 A.M.	4 min, 23 sec	106%
Visibility: See front of book				
Apr. 29, 1995	a	12:32 P.M.	6 min, 37 sec	95%
Visibility: Ecuador, Peru, Colombia, Brazil; partial in southern South America, Central America, Caribbean, southern Mexico				
Oct. 23–24, 1995	t	11:32 P.M.	2 min, 9 sec	102%
Visibility: See front of book				
Apr. 17, 1996	p	5:37 P.M.	—	88%
Visibility: New Zealand, southern Pacific				
Oct. 12, 1996	p	9:02 A.M.	—	76%
Visibility: Europe, northern Africa, North Atlantic				
Mar. 8, 1997	t	8:24 P.M.	2 min, 50 sec	104%
Visibility: See front of book				
Sep. 1, 1997	p	7:04 P.M.	—	90%
Visibility: Australia, New Zealand, Pacific				
Feb. 26, 1998	t	12:28 P.M.	4 min, 9 sec	104%
Visibility: See front of book				
Aug. 21, 1998	a	9:06 P.M.	3 min, 14 sec	97%
Visibility: See front of book				
Feb. 16, 1999	a	1:34 A.M.	0 min, 40 sec	99%
Visibility: Indian Ocean, western and northern Australia; partial in southern Africa, Australia, Indonesia, Antarctica				
Aug. 11, 1999	t	6:03 P.M.	2 min, 23 sec	103%
Visibility: See front of book and diagram on page 127				
Feb. 5, 2000	p	7:49 A.M.	—	58%
Visibility: Antarctica				
July 1, 2000	p	2:33 P.M.	—	48%
Visibility: South Pacific				
July 30, 2000	p	9:13 P.M.	—	60%
Visibility: the Arctic, Alaska, northern USSR				
Dec. 25, 2000	p	12:35 P.M.	—	72%
Visibility: Canada, USA, Mexico, Caribbean				

p = partial; t = total; a = annular; min = minutes, sec = seconds

Dates, Duration, and Visibility of Lunar Eclipses

Unlike solar eclipses, lunar eclipses can be observed with considerably greater frequency in any given country. The simple reason for this is that every lunar eclipse is visible on the entire dark side of Earth. However, fascinating lunar eclipses are rarer than solar eclipses, as the table below, which lists all the lunar eclipses over a ten-year period, shows. It lists only 14 lunar eclipses, whereas the table on pages 110 and 111 lists 23 solar eclipses for the years 1991 to 2000.

Earth, like the Moon, projects a shadow into space that consists of an umbra and a penumbra, but only the umbra is of interest in connection with lunar eclipses. When the Moon traverses Earth's penumbra, this is difficult to see from Earth. That is why the table below includes only eclipses during which the Moon travels through Earth's umbra.

When the fully lit disk of the Moon (the full moon) moves completely into Earth's umbra, a total eclipse occurs; when it moves past the umbra's center to the north or south and the umbra covers it only partially, it is a partial eclipse. (The exact extent of all the total lunar eclipses up to and including the year 2000 are shown on the back flap and

Lunar Eclipses: When and Where They Are Visible

Date	Type	Beginning	End	Extent
Dec. 21, 1991	p	5:00 A.M.	6:06 A.M.	9%
Visibility: USA, Canada, South America, Pacific, eastern USSR				
May 14–15, 1992	p	10:27 P.M.	1:27 A.M.	69%
Visibility: USA, Canada, South America, Africa, parts of Europe				
Dec. 9, 1992	t	4:59 P.M.	8:29 P.M.	127%
Visibility: See back of book				
June 4, 1993	t	6:11 A.M.	9:50 A.M.	157%
Visibility: See back of book				
Nov. 28–29, 1993	t	11:40 P.M.	3:12 A.M.	109%
Visibility: See back of book				
May 24, 1994	p	9:38 P.M.	11:23 P.M.	25%
Visibility: USA, Canada, South America, parts of Europe, Africa				
Apr. 15, 1995	p	6:41 A.M.	7:55 A.M.	12%
Visibility: Australia, New Zealand, Pacific, Japan, Indonesia				
Apr. 3, 1996	t	5:21 P.M.	8:59 P.M.	138%
Visibility: See back of book				
Sep. 26, 1996	t	8:12 P.M.	11:36 P.M.	124%
Visibility: See back of book				
Mar. 23–24, 1997	p	9:58 P.M.	1:22 A.M.	92%
Visibility: Canada, USA, South America, Europe, parts of Africa				
Sep. 16, 1997	t	12:08 P.M.	3:25 P.M.	120%
Visibility: See back of book				
July 28, 1999	p	5:22 A.M.	7:45 A.M.	40%
Visibility: Australia, New Zealand, East Asia, Pacific				
Jan. 20–21, 2000	t	10:01 P.M.	1:26 A.M.	133%
Visibility: See back of book				
July 16, 2000	t	6:57 A.M.	10:54 A.M.	177%
Visibility: See back of book				

p = partial; t = total

inside cover.) Because Earth rotates, there is always a wide border zone in which the Moon either rises or sets during an eclipse.

To a hypothetical observer on the Moon, a lunar eclipse would appear the way a solar eclipse appears to us. For just as Earth plunges into the Moon's shadow during a solar eclipse, the Moon is engulfed by Earth's shadow as Earth moves between it and the Sun. Seen from Earth, the brightly lit disk of the Moon begins to darken more and more until it gradually is extinguished. But— and this is the crucial and really intriguing part of it all—the Moon's disk does not

fade away completely but remains faintly visible through Earth's shadow even at the height of a total eclipse. This is because of Earth's atmosphere, which refracts the Sun's light and redirects some of it into Earth's shadow, where it strikes the Moon's surface and is reflected by it. Because this is true especially of the red spectrum of the Sun's light, the Moon often glows in a dark, coppery red during a total eclipse. However, this varies from eclipse to eclipse; the color depends primarily on the dust particles in Earth's atmosphere (see photo on front cover of book).

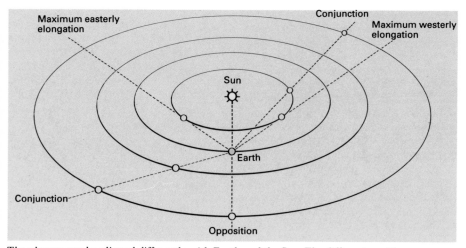

The planets can be aligned differently with Earth and the Sun. The different positions are called opposition, conjunction, and elongation (see page 114).

The Planets Appear in the Constellations of the Zodiac

The planets are lit up by the Sun and reflect the light toward Earth. Because of their proximity to Earth, they appear to move. This movement is always along the ecliptic, that is, the path the Sun seems to take across the sky in the course of the year. The ecliptic is entered in the star maps as a dotted line, so that it will be easy to find the

planets in the sky. Planets are always very bright and they are always found along the ecliptic (see page 15). Their various positions in relation to Earth and the Sun are shown in the diagram above.

The famous constellations of the zodiac are lined up along the ecliptic (see pages 15–16). The planets therefore can show up only within these 13 constellations, which makes it even easier to spot them.

The appearance of the planets depends on whether they are closer to or farther away from the Sun than Earth (see diagram on page 17).

Mercury and Venus, the so-called inferior planets, are closer to the Sun than Earth is; the "superior" planets Mars, Jupiter, and Saturn are farther away.

Because Mercury and Venus orbit so closely to the Sun, they never can move very far away from it. They therefore are visible only in the evening in the western sky shortly after sunset or early in the morning in the eastern sky just before sunrise. The best position to observe them in is when their distance from the Sun, which is measured in degrees of an angle, is greatest. (The times when this is the case—the so-called *maximum elongation*—are given for Mercury in the table on pages 114 and 115 and for Venus in the table on page 116.)

Mars, Jupiter, and Saturn move around the Sun outside of Earth's orbit. In Earth's sky they can be opposite to the Sun, in a position where they are said to be at *opposition*. The times when this happens are given in the table on page 117. When one of these three planets is at opposition, it means that it is in its best position for observation because the planet is then in the sky all night. It rises approximately at sunset and sets when the Sun rises again.

The planets move across the sky at different rates. Mercury is the fastest; Saturn, the slowest. That is why their positions relative to each other keep changing. Often two or more planets converge in one of the constellations of the zodiac and then are aligned with each other exactly in a north-south direction. This is called a *conjunction* (see diagram on page 113). Planetary conjunctions are important celestial events; the sky appears different and striking because several planets are added to these constellations. (The most interesting planetary conjunctions for the years 1992 to 2000 are shown in small diagrams accompanying the descriptions of all the celestial events for that time span, starting on page 119.)

Mercury Appears Only Briefly

Mercury is the most difficult planet to observe both in the evening and in the morning. (The table lists only the times when this planet is particularly far east of the Sun and is thus visible in the evening.) The tropical countries are the best place from which to watch Mercury because dusk is so brief there and the planet is still relatively high above the horizon in the west when darkness falls. In zones farther north or south—that is, especially for the star map series N I (50 degrees north)—Mercury can be seen only with difficulty. The table for Mercury therefore indicates whether the planet is in an unfavorable position for observation anywhere on Earth or whether it can be seen better from the Northern or the Southern Hemisphere. These remarks are

Mercury 1991–2000

Year	Evening Sky (Constellation)	Visibility
1991	March–April (Pisces)	north
	July–August (Leo)	south
	November (Scorpius)	south
1992	March (Pisces)	unfavorable
	July (Cancer)	south
	October–November (Libra/Scorpius)	south
1993	February (Aquarius)	unfavorable
	June (Gemini)	south
	October (Libra)	south

Mercury 1991–2000

Year	Evening Sky (Constellation)	Visibility
1994	January–February (Aquarius)	unfavorable
	May–June (Taurus, Gemini)	north
	September (Virgo)	south
1995	January (Capricornus)	north
	May (Taurus)	north
	September (Virgo)	south
1996	January (Sagittarius/Capricornus)	unfavorable
	April (Aries)	north
	August (Leo/Virgo)	south
	December (Sagittarius)	south
1997	April (Aries)	north
	July–August (Leo)	south
	November–December (Scorpius)	south
1998	March (Pisces)	north
	July (Cancer/Leo)	south
	November (Scorpius)	south
1999	February–March (Pisces)	unfavorable
	June–July (Gemini/Cancer)	south
	October (Libra)	south
2000	February (Aquarius)	unfavorable
	June (Gemini)	south
	September–October (Virgo/Libra)	south

of no consequence for the equatorial regions. There Mercury is clearly visible in the evening in the west at any of the times indicated; however, one always has to look for it low on the horizon. (See also page 137.)

Mercury's Transits

When Mercury passes between Earth and the Sun, it happens once in a while that the planet passes directly in front of the solar disk. This is a kind of mini-eclipse with Mercury instead of the Moon covering part of the Sun. However, Mercury is so far away from Earth that it appears only as a tiny black dot against the Sun's disk, which is 150 times larger than that of the planet. During this decade, two of these rare Mercury transits will occur, but watching them is both difficult and dangerous. The only truly safe way is to project the Sun's image through a small telescope or through small binoculars onto a sheet of white paper and follow Mercury's transit there.

On November 5, 1993, between 10:07 and 11:47 P.M. a Mercury transit will be visible from Australia, Indonesia, China, Japan, India, and New Zealand. Another one will occur on November 15, 1999, from 3:16 to 4:08 P.M. This one will be visible from New Zealand, Hawaii, eastern Australia, the west coast of North and South America, and the Pacific Ocean.

Venus, the Morning and Evening Star

Unlike Mercury, Venus can move much farther away from the Sun and consequently can stay in the sky much later in the evening after sunset and appear again much earlier before sunrise. It is also the brightest heavenly object apart from the Sun and the Moon and is therefore often visible before sunset, when it is still daylight. The table (on page 116) includes not only evening appearances but also those in the morning because Venus is often the only celestial body to be seen on

Venus 1991-2000

Year	Evening star	Morning star
	(maximum elongation from the Sun and constellations during the month of maximum elongation)	
1991	January–August (6/13, Gemini, Cancer, Leo)	September–December (11/2, Leo, Virgo)
1992	September–December	January–March
1993	January–March (1/19, Aquarius, Pisces)	April–October (6/10, Aries, Taurus)
1994	March–October (8/24, Virgo, Libra)	December
1995	November–December	January–May (1/13, Libra, Scorpius, Sagittarius)
1996	January–May (4/1, Taurus)	July–December (8/20, Taurus, Gemini, Cancer)
1997	June–December (11/6, Sagittarius)	—
1998	—	February–August (3/27, Capricornus, Aquarius)
1999	January–August (6/11, Gemini, Cancer, Leo)	September–December (10/30, Leo)
2000	August–December	January–March

one's way to work or when one first looks at the sky in the morning. Its still, white luminosity makes it a point of light that can't be missed. (See also page 151.)

Mars, the Red Planet

The planet Mars can come very close to Earth. It is second nearest to Earth, after Venus. Its visibility therefore follows an irregular pattern, too. There are years when it is never found at opposition, and there are years when it does not appear in the evening sky at all but only in the morning (see table on page 117). Mars glows with a reddish

light; it is always fainter than Venus and almost always fainter than Jupiter as well, but generally exceeds even the most luminous "fixed" stars in brightness. Its light has a reddish cast to it that is caused by extensive deserts that cover huge areas of its surface. (See also page 137.)

Jupiter in a Yellowish Light

Jupiter, which is by far the largest planet of the solar system, shines with a clearly visible, yellowish light. It is very bright, constituting the second most luminous celestial object, after Venus (and excepting the Sun and the Moon). Only on very rare occasions does Mars outshine it for a few weeks during an opposition with exceptionally favorable conditions (this will not, however, happen at all during this decade). Jupiter's orbit around the Sun takes about 12 years, and it therefore moves along the sky from one zodiacal constellation to the next with each opposition, as the table on page 117 clearly shows. (See also page 136.)

Saturn, the Planet in White

Saturn is the slowest moving of the planets that can be observed with the unaided eye. It is also the least bright, although it is still on a par with the brightest stars in the sky. In looking for Saturn, one is helped not only by the fact that the planet always appears exactly on the ecliptic but also—and even more—by its steady light that barely flickers at all (see page 17 and the photo on pages 6–7). The famous rings of Saturn can be seen only with the aid of a telescope with a magnification of at least 40. Between 1994 and 1996 the rings will not be visible at all because they are tipped toward Earth in such a way that they are on edge to our line of sight, and thus too narrow to be seen. (See also page 146.)

When the Planets Can Be Seen

Mars 1990–2000

Year	Opposition	Constellation at Opposition	Visible in the evening sky
1990	November 27	Taurus	September–December
1991	—	—	January–July (Taurus–Cancer)
1992	—	—	November–December (Gemini)
1993	January 7	Gemini	January–August
1994	—	—	(only in the morning before sunrise)
1995	February 12	Leo	January–October
1996	—	—	(only in the morning before sunrise)
1997	March 17	Leo/Virgo	February–November
1998	—	—	(only in the morning before sunrise)
1999	April 24	Virgo	March–December
2000	—	Aquarius	January–February

Jupiter 1991–2000

1991	January 29	Cancer	January–June
1992	February 29	Leo	February–July
1993	March 30	Virgo	March–August
1994	April 30	Libra/Virgo	May–September
1995	June 1	Ophiuchus	June–October
1996	July 4	Sagittarius	July–December
1997	August 9	Capricornus	August–December
1998	September 16	Aquarius/Pisces	January/September–December
1999	October 23	Pisces/Aries	January–February/October–December
2000	November 28	Taurus	January–March/November–December

Saturn 1991–2000

1991	July 27	Sagittarius/Capricornus	July–December
1992	August 7	Capricornus	August–December
1993	August 19	Capricornus/Aquarius	January/August–December
1994	September 1	Aquarius	January/September–December
1995	September 14	Aquarius/Pisces	January/September–December
1996	September 26	Pisces	January–February/October–December
1997	October 10	Pisces	January–February/October–December
1998	October 23	Pisces/Aries	January–March/October–December
1999	November 6	Aries	January–March/November–December
2000	November 19	Aries/Taurus	January–April/November–December

The total lunar eclipse of August 16/17, 1989. After totality (above left), the edge of Earth's inner shadow (umbra) can be seen traveling across the lunar surface.

Astronomical Calendar 1992–2000

1992

The year begins with an annular solar eclipse on **January** 4. The eclipse can be seen in Earth's Southern Hemisphere. No planets are visible in the evening.

Jupiter moves into our field of view in **February**. It becomes visible after midnight in the constellation Leo in the eastern sky. On February 29, Jupiter is at opposition to the Sun. From about 6 A.M. on, shortly before sunrise, a spectacular configuration of planets becomes visible in the morning sky in the constellation Capricornus. Venus, Mars, and Saturn gather there in closest proximity to each other (see diagram 1 and 2, page 119).

By **March**, Jupiter has become the dominant planet in the evening sky and is among the most striking objects to be seen in the east after sunset.

Jupiter continues to solidify its position in the sky during **April** and holds it throughout **May**; it will continue to stand in the constellation Leo for the rest of the year.

In **June**, Jupiter retains its dominant position, becoming visible in the southwestern sky as soon as the Sun sets. On June 14, inhabitants of South and North America experience a partial lunar eclipse.

In **July**, Jupiter is joined by swiftly moving Mercury low in the western sky. At the beginning of the month, Mercury can be seen in the Southern Hemisphere shortly after sunset.

In **August**, Jupiter gives way to Saturn; Jupiter is too close to the Sun to remain visible, whereas Saturn, being at opposition on August 7 in the constellation Capricornus, rises in the eastern sky at sunset.

In **September**, Venus makes lengthy evening appearances, shining forth in the west as the brightest point in the sky immediately after sunset. Saturn remains the planet of the first half of the night.

October brings two uncommon celestial events: On October 27, the Moon eclipses Mercury, and on the October 28, it similarly hides Venus. Both of these events can be seen from North America and from the Atlantic Ocean. The October sky displays Saturn high in the south in the evening, Venus as the evening star in the west, and, at the end of the month and visible from the southern half of the globe, Mercury low in the west after sunset.

Mercury continues to be briefly visible at the beginning of **November**, while Venus and Saturn move toward each other, lending an unusual appearance to the western sky during the evening hours.

This convergent movement of Venus and Saturn

(1)   2/19/92

(2)   2/29/92

(3)   12/21/92

reaches its peak in **December**, when, on December 21, the two planets dominate the western sky looking like a double star (see diagram 3, page 119). December also closes the year 1992 with two eclipses, one a total lunar eclipse on December 9, visible from Europe; the other a

1992/1993

partial solar eclipse on December 23, which passes across northeastern Asia and the northern Pacific.

1993

Venus, which is approaching its period of greatest brightness, is the dominant point of light in the **January** sky. It is the planet of the early evening hours, whereas the later evening and the night belong to Mars, which is found at opposition on January 7 in the constellation Gemini.

Mars and Venus still rule over the **February** sky, although Venus gradually is preparing to exit and can by the end of the month be seen for only about an hour after sunset.

In **March,** Mars is the only planet in the evening sky, but only until the end of the month, when Jupiter also turns up, appearing in the eastern sky at sunset.

During **April,** the evening sky belongs to Jupiter and Mars. Mars is clearly farther west in the constellation Gemini, with Jupiter appearing more to the east in the constellation Virgo.

Mars and Jupiter continue to be just as prominently apparent in the evening sky during **May.** A partial solar eclipse occurs on May 21 and can be watched by observers in North America and northern Europe.

In **June**, Mars and Jupiter, whose distance from each other keeps shrinking, are joined by Mercury. In the middle of the month, observers in the Southern Hemisphere can see this small planet in the evening sky for three quarters of an hour in the constellation Virgo. On June 4, there is a total lunar eclipse (visible from eastern Asia and Australia).

In **July,** Jupiter and Mars are no longer in the sky all night but set before midnight. By this time, Jupiter has become noticeably brighter than Mars.

In **August,** Saturn shows up in the evening sky for the first time this year; on August 14 it is at opposition. In the meantime the distance between Jupiter and Mars has diminished so much that these two planets appear lined up in a close conjunction in the evening sky for about two hours on **September** 7 (see diagram 4, page 120). Saturn remains the planet of the first half of the night.

In **October,** sky watchers in the Southern Hemisphere have the rare opportunity of seeing a close conjunction of Mercury and Mars twice in a row. The two planets can be seen together in the evening sky in the constellation Libra (see diagrams 5 and 6, pages 120 and 121). For those watching from the northern half of the globe, there is only one planet to see, Saturn,

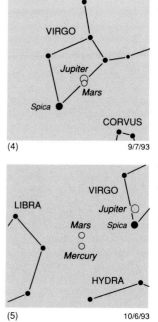

(4)   9/7/93

(5)   10/6/93

which appears at sunset in the southeast.

November brings a number of interesting celestial events. The first one occurs on November 5. It is one of the rare Mercury transits, when the planet moves across the solar disk (see page 115). This is followed on November 13 by a partial solar eclipse that is visible only in the southernmost zone of the Southern Hemisphere. On November 28–29, observers in North and South America, western Europe, and northeastern Asia can witness a total lunar eclipse. In the evening sky, Saturn is once again the only planet to be seen.

1993/1994

OPHIUCHUS

Mars ○
Mercury ○

Antares
SCORPIUS
LIBRA
(6)   10/28/93

December brings the year to a close with only one easily visible planet in the evening sky, Saturn, which can be seen in the border area between Capricornus and Aquarius but leaves the sky again toward 10 P.M.

1994
The months **January, February,** and **March** pass without special events. The only planets to be seen are Saturn in the west after sunset during the first half of January and, at the end of January and beginning of February, Mercury low in the western evening sky.

Not until **April** does Venus gradually begin to appear as the evening star in the west. During the night from April 12–13 Venus is covered up by the Moon, but this can be seen only in the high Arctic latitudes on the northern half of the globe.

May brings a number of celestial events of interest. First of all, Venus grows more

and more prominent as the evening star; and, after Venus sets, Jupiter adds brightness to the sky since it was at opposition on April 30. On May 10 there is an annular solar eclipse, which is followed on May 24 by a partial lunar eclipse. Both of these eclipses can be seen from North, Central, and South America.

June starts out with Mercury in a favorable viewing position in the constellations Taurus and Gemini. There it is visible in the evening in the western sky for sky watchers in the Northern Hemisphere. Venus glows ever brighter as the evening star until about three hours after sunset, and Jupiter dominates the first half of the night in the constellation Virgo.

July brings no major changes. Venus and Jupiter move visibly closer to each other, and Venus is by far the brightest point of light in the sky.

During **August,** Venus is at its greatest brightness for the year 1994. But Jupiter, which now can be found as early as at sunset in the southern sky, almost matches Venus in luminosity.

In **September**, the two planets converge closer and closer in the constellation Libra without, however, coming into conjunction. Both planets now remain visible in the western sky for only

about three hours after sunset. But at the beginning of the month, making up for their lessening presence in the sky, Saturn turns up in the east in the constellation Aquarius (at opposition on September 1). During the last two weeks of the month, Mercury glows in the westerly evening sky in a position that is quite favorable for observation from the southern half of the globe.

Shortly before ending its appearances in the evening sky in **October**, Jupiter is covered up on October 7 by the Moon, an event that can be observed, however, only from the southernmost zones of the southern half of the globe. Mercury vanishes from the sky during the first week of October, as does Venus in the middle of the month, leaving Saturn as the only planet of the first half of the night. Saturn is already high in the southeastern sky in the constellation Aquarius by the time the Sun sets.

On **November** 3, a total solar eclipse occurs. This event, too, is visible only from the southern half of the globe. Otherwise Saturn is the only planet that is easy to see both in November and **December**. It shows up in the evening sky in the constellation Aquarius.

1995

1995

Mercury and Saturn are the only planets visible in the evening during **January**. In the temperate latitudes of the Northern Hemisphere, Mercury appears in the western sky in the middle of the month. Also in the west, low in the sky, Saturn can be spotted after sunset in the constellation Aquarius.

In **February**, Mars returns to the evening sky. It is at opposition on February 12.

From **March** until May, Mars is the only planet in the evening sky, gleaming with a conspicuous reddish tint in the constellations Cancer and Leo.

Two eclipses take place during **April**. On April 15, the Moon appears partially eclipsed in Australia and the nearby Pacific states, and on April 29, Central and South America experience an annular solar eclipse.

In addition to Mars, which glows in the evening sky, **May** also briefly displays Mercury to observers in the Northern Hemisphere. In the middle of the month, this planet appears in the evening in the northwestern sky.

In **June**, Mars, which shows up soon after sunset in the southwest, is joined by Jupiter. Jupiter is at opposition on June 1, so that it will be the most conspicuous point of light in the evening sky during the coming months.

During **July** and **August**, the distance between Mars and Jupiter in the evening sky diminishes noticeably, with Jupiter exceeding Mars more and more in brightness. On August 30, Mars is eclipsed by the Moon (visible from the Pacific area).

In **September**, three planets are visible in the evening. They are (about one hour after sunset) Mars deep in the western sky, Jupiter in the southwest, and Saturn in the east, where it is at opposition on September 14 in the constellation Aquarius.

There is no change in the position of the planets during **October**. However, Jupiter and Mars, which are moving closer together in the west, are setting very early. On October 23–24, there is a spectacular total solar eclipse over the Pacific Ocean.

Another impressive celestial sight is the multiple conjunction of the planets Mars, Jupiter, and Venus in **November** in the constellations Scorpius and Ophiuchus. The three planets are found very close together from November 16–22 and shine like a threefold star shortly after sunset, though very low in the western sky (see diagrams 7, 8, and 9, page 122). Otherwise Saturn is the dominant planet of the evening sky, a position it maintains into **December**. It is now in the constellation Aquarius, where it appears in the south-

(7)   11/16/95

(8)   11/19/95

(9)   11/22/95

west after sunset. Venus is visible as the evening star in the constellation Sagittarius until two hours after sunset.

1996

At the beginning of **January**, stargazers in the temperate latitudes of the Northern Hemisphere can watch Mercury in the evening in the western sky. Venus is increasingly asserting its stature as the evening star and heading with accelerating speed toward Saturn, which is positioned somewhat farther east, in the constellation Aquarius.

February brings this situation to a climax when the two planets come into conjunction on February 3 (see diagram 10, page 123). The two planets shine together in the southwest after sunset, with Venus's brightness clearly exceeding that of Saturn. On February 22, Venus is eclipsed by the Moon (visible only from the Pacific area).

From **March** on, Venus is the only planet left in the evening sky. Its brightness is still increasing noticeably, and by the end of the month it sets as late as 11 P.M.

During **April**, Venus continues to be the only planet in the evening sky. It increases even more in brightness and one probably will be able to detect it in the west in the daytime sky before the Sun even sets. The absence of planets (other than Venus) is compensated for by two eclipses. On April 3, there is a total lunar eclipse, and on April 17, a partial solar eclipse can be seen over the

South Pacific. In addition, Mercury can be spotted in the Northern Hemisphere during the last week of April, appearing shortly after sunset for a maximum of half an hour in the constellation Aries.

During **May**, Venus still retains its dominant position in the evening sky. But it sets earlier and earlier while the Sun sets later and later, so that its period of visibility becomes briefer and briefer.

In **June**, no planets are visible either in the evening or the first half of the night. But in the morning, shortly before sunrise at about 3 A.M., a spectacular gathering of the planets Mars, Venus, and Mercury takes place (see diagrams 11, 12, 13, and 14 on pages 123 and 124). In the period between May 31 and June 30, these planets are in conjunction with each other four times.

Nothing of comparable excitement happens in **July**. The most noteworthy event of this month is the appearance of Jupiter in the evening sky and its moving into opposition to the Sun on July 4.

During **August**, Jupiter, appearing in the constellation Sagittarius, remains the only planet of the first half of the night. Observers on the southern half of the globe also can watch Mercury in the evening, when it occupies a very favorable position in the con-

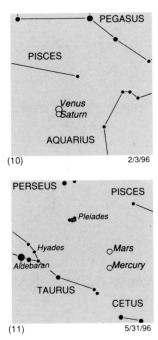

(10)　　　　　　　　2/3/96

(11)　　　　　　　　5/31/96

stellations Leo and Virgo in the western sky.

By **September**, Jupiter, which is in the constellation Sagittarius, has moved into the southern sky by the time darkness falls, where it remains the only visible planet in the evening.

It is not until the end of September that Saturn joins Jupiter. On September 25, Saturn is at opposition and rises in the sky at sunset, when Jupiter has already arrived in the southwest. On September 26, a total lunar eclipse can be observed from North and South America as well as from Africa and Europe.

1996/1997

(12)   6/14/96

(13)   6/23/96

(14)   6/30/96

In **October**, too, Jupiter and Saturn are the only visible planets during the first half of the night. Jupiter is in Sagittarius; Saturn, in Pisces. On October 12, there is a partial solar eclipse that is visible from Europe and also from North America and Africa.

In **November**, Jupiter and Saturn still are visible in the evening hours, with Jupiter still in Sagittarius and Saturn in Pisces.

The same situation persists into **December**. Observers on the southern half of the globe also can glimpse swift Mercury in the middle of the month. Jupiter remains visible very low in the western sky only until the middle of December, so that by the end of the year, Saturn, which appears in the evening in the southwestern sky, is the only planet left.

1997

In **January**, Saturn is the only visible planet. It is in the constellation Pisces in the southwestern evening sky.

February brings no change except that Saturn exits earlier, disappearing in the west about three hours after sunset.

March, on the other hand, brings three celestial events of interest. On March 9, there is a total solar eclipse, and on March 23–24, the Moon disappears partially in Earth's shadow. On March 17, Mars is at opposition to the Sun, thus becoming the only planet visible during the first half of the night. It appears at sunset in the east in the constellation Leo.

In **April**, Mercury briefly appears to observers in the Northern Hemisphere. They can see the planet low in the western evening sky until the middle of the month. Mars further solidifies its dominant position in the sky, continuing to shine very brightly in the constellation Leo.

This situation remains unchanged during **May**. Not until the last days of May does Venus appear low in the west as the evening star.

In **June**, Venus is able to assert its position as the dominant evening star more firmly, but it sets long before Mars, which doesn't set into the west until about midnight. On June 13, Mars is covered by the Moon, an event that can be observed from Africa and from the Indian Ocean.

In **July**, Mars and Venus are still competing for dominance in the evening sky (Venus is in Cancer and Leo; Mars, in Virgo). At the end of the month they are joined—for observers in the Southern Hemisphere—by Mercury, which can be spotted close to Venus, also in the constellation Leo.

Mercury continues to occupy a position favorable for evening viewing during early **August**. Venus and Mars, whose visibility remains practically unchanged from July, are joined after midnight by Jupiter in the east. Jupiter is at opposition on August 9.

Venus, Mars, and Jupiter are the dominant planets of the evening sky during **Sep-**

1997/1998

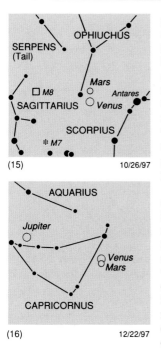

(15)   10/26/97

(16)   12/22/97

tember. Venus and Mars now are moving along converging southwesterly courses in the constellation Libra, while Jupiter glows east of them in the constellation Capricornus. Two eclipses take place during this month: On September 1 the Sun appears partially eclipsed over Australia and the southwestern Pacific, and on September 16, people watching from Europe, Africa, and Asia can witness a total lunar eclipse.

In **October**, Mars and Venus meet in an impressive conjunction in the constellations Scorpius and Ophiuchus in the western sky. The two planets remain in the same

position until December, moving apart only slightly (see diagrams 15 and 16, left). Also in October they are joined in the sky by Saturn (it is at opposition on October 10), so that during the months of October, **November**, and December, the evening and night sky is graced by an unusually impressive array of planets.

From October until **December**, all five planets visible to the naked eye can be seen in the sky in the evening, though Mercury's appearance is delayed until late November. Saturn shines in the constellation Pisces; Jupiter, in Capricornus; Mars and Venus move along next to each other in Sagittarius; and Mercury can be found in the constellations Scorpius and Sagittarius in late November and into early December.

1998

On **January** 5, Saturn is eclipsed when, for observers in South Africa and countries bordering the Indian Ocean, it disappears behind the Moon. Saturn is the only planet in the evening sky (except during the first half of January when Jupiter still keeps it company), and even it stays visible only until shortly before midnight.

On **February** 1, Saturn is again eclipsed by the Moon. Otherwise it can be seen in

the evening sky in the constellation Pisces, though only until about 11 P.M. Sky watchers are compensated for the absence of other planets by a total solar eclipse on February 26, which is visible from Central America and the northern part of South America.

On **March** 1, Saturn disappears behind the Moon once again, but this can be seen only from the southern parts of the globe. Saturn then remains visible only for the first half of the month, low in the western sky. There it appears together with Mercury in the constellation Pisces (only for observers in the Northern Hemisphere). Then the sky of the evening and the first half of the night is devoid of planets from **April** until September—an unusually long period. However, the morning sky presents planets in a spectacular position during both April and **May** as Venus moves into conjunction with Jupiter and Saturn (see diagrams 17 and 18, page 126). At the end of **June** and in **July**, Mercury turns up after sunset (in the Southern Hemisphere) deep in the western sky in the constellations Cancer and Leo. During July, Mercury's appearance lasts for only an hour. Another event worth mention is an annular solar eclipse on **August** 21, visible from Southeast Asia, Australia, and the Pacific.

1998/1999

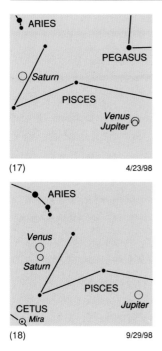

(17) 4/23/98

(18) 9/29/98

During this period, all the planets are gathered in the morning sky. They rise long after midnight and can be seen until dawn breaks.

Starting in **September**, Jupiter, which is at opposition on September 16, rises again in the evening sky.

Jupiter is joined in **October** by Saturn, which also moves into this favorable position on October 24. The two planets are relatively close to each other; Jupiter is the brighter of the pair and stands west of Saturn.

Jupiter and Saturn remain the only two planets visible in the evening sky during **November**. Only in the

Southern Hemisphere can Mercury be seen as well in the middle of the month in the constellation Scorpius in the western sky. On November 17, an unusually heavy stream of meteors may appear, the Leonids (see page 139).

On **December** 25, Jupiter (in the constellation Aquarius) is once more covered up by the Moon. Apart from Saturn (in the constellation Pisces), it is the only planet to show up in the evening sky; both can be seen at sunset, toward the south.

1999

Jupiter and Saturn dominate the evening sky in **January**. Jupiter, the brighter of the two planets, is farther to the west. Shortly after sunset, Venus also appears as the evening star in the west.

During **February**, Venus consolidates its position as the brightest celestial body. Appearing in the evening, it moves toward Jupiter, with which it is in conjunction on February 23, and then continues on toward Saturn (see diagram 19, page 127). On February 16, an annular solar eclipse can be observed over South Africa, Australia, and Southeast Asia.

At the beginning of **March**, Mercury can be glimpsed briefly in the evening in the southern parts of

the Northern Hemisphere. However, viewing conditions are far from favorable. Venus's moving away from Jupiter and toward Saturn, which it reaches on March 20, is much more spectacular. Venus, Jupiter, and Saturn form a conspicuous triangle in the western sky throughout the month (see diagrams 19 and 20, page 127).

Of this planetary trio, only Venus is left by **April**. It shines in the western sky as the evening star for more than four hours after sunset. Jupiter and Saturn are close to the Sun, invisible in the daytime sky. At the end of April, Mars returns to the evening sky. It is at opposition on April 24.

During **May**, Venus is visible as the evening star in the constellations Taurus and Gemini. Mars also shows up farther to the east in Virgo.

In **June**, Venus grows toward its greatest brightness, at which point it can be seen even before sunset in the daytime sky. At the end of the month, sky watchers in the Southern Hemisphere also can watch Mercury's progress from Gemini to Cancer in a position favorable for viewing. Mars stays in the constellation Virgo during the whole month.

During **July**, Venus and Mars continue as the planets of the first half of the night. The distance between them

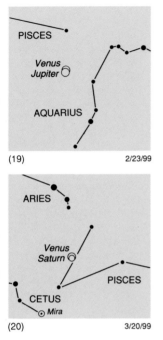

PISCES

Venus
Jupiter ○

AQUARIUS

(19)   2/23/99

ARIES

Venus
Saturn ○

PISCES

CETUS
⊙ Mira

(20)   3/20/99

September shows practically no changes in the sky from the conditions that prevailed in the previous month. Mars, the only planet in the evening sky at this time, moves into the constellations Scorpius and Ophiuchus.

In **October**, new planets appear in the evening sky. From the Southern Hemisphere, Mercury can be observed in the evening during the second half of the month in the western sky in the constellation Libra. Mars, looking practically unchanged from the previous months, sets in the constellation Sagittarius. Jupiter and Saturn, which have in the meantime moved very close together in the constellation Aries, enter the sky almost simultaneously in the east around midnight.

In **November**, Mars, Jupiter, and Saturn can be seen clearly in the evening sky starting at sunset. Mars, which already has moved far into the west, has diminished much in brightness but is still definitely present as a point of light in the constellation Sagittarius. Jupiter and Saturn appear considerably brighter in Aries. On November 15, people watching in the Pacific region can witness a spectacular celestial event when Mercury passes in front of the Sun's disk (see page 115).

In **December**, Mars, Jupiter, and Saturn are still in the evening sky. Mars is in Capricornus, while Jupiter and Saturn appear in Aries.

2000

January shows the planets Mars, Jupiter, and Saturn in the evening sky. The three planets are drawing closer together, Jupiter and Saturn in Aries and Mars farther to the west in Aquarius. On January 21, observers in Europe and North and South America can witness a total lunar eclipse.

In **February**, Mars, Jupiter, and Saturn—all three still visible in the evening sky—are joined by Mercury, though the latter can be spotted only under exceptionally favorable viewing conditions in the western sky, just barely above the horizon.

During **March**, Mars, Jupiter, and Saturn are in the evening sky, moving toward a spectacular conjunction that will take place the next month.

These developments come to a peak in **April**, when the three planets move into conjunction with each other in Aries (see diagram 21, page 128). This uncommon meeting of the three planets is, however, visible only immediately after sunset, low in the western sky.

By **May,** the planets have vanished from the evening sky and now accompany the Sun across the daytime sky.

gradually decreases. Venus is the brightest spot in the sky while Mars begins to grow gradually dimmer. On July 28, there is a partial lunar eclipse that is visible from the countries of the Pacific region.

By **August**, only Mars is left in the evening sky. By the time dusk falls it is already high in the southern sky, in front of the stars that make up Libra. On August 11, observers in North America as well as in Europe and northern Africa have a chance to witness a total solar eclipse, an eclipse that will be for Europe one of the most spectacular celestial events of the entire twentieth century.

On the last day of the month, there is a rare conjunction of Jupiter and Saturn in the morning sky—what may be regarded as a reenactment of the appearance of the famous Star of Bethlehem. According to the most plausible explanation that has been put forth to date, the Star of Bethlehem as described in the Bible was actually a conjunction of the planets Jupiter and Saturn that took place in the year 7 B.C.

In **June**, Mercury is the only planet to be seen in the evening during the early part of the month. It appears briefly in the constellation Gemini after sunset.

During **July**, the evening sky is devoid of planets. But there are three eclipses during this month, an unusually large number for one month. The first one, a partial solar eclipse, takes place on July 1 and is visible in southern parts of South America and in the

southern Pacific. On July 16, a total lunar eclipse can be viewed in Australia and Antarctica. On July 30, the Sun will be partially obscured by the Moon, an event that can be observed from northern Asia and North America.

In **August**, Venus appears shortly after sunset in the west.

During **September**, Venus consolidates its position as the evening star, setting gradually later and later after sunset (in the constellation Virgo) until December.

At the end of September and the beginning of **October**, Venus is joined in the evening sky by Mercury, which enhances the area of the constellation Libra for observers in the Southern Hemisphere.

Starting in **November**, Jupiter and then Saturn also return to the evening sky. They can be found in the constellation Taurus. Together with Venus, they are the planets of the first half of the night during **December**.

The second millenium A.D. concludes with Venus shining for about four hours as the evening star in the constellation Capricornus. Jupiter and Saturn are visible for the entire night. They stand close together in the constellation Taurus, looking like a kind of double star and thus adding to the splendor of the night sky at the close of our millenium.

Star tracks around the south celestial pole.

Lexicon of Celestial Bodies

Achernar

Achernar is the ninth brightest star in the sky. Its name comes from the Arabic expression Al Ahir al Nahr (the end of the river), which was later corrupted into the present form. The name refers to the star's position in the constellation Eridanus, a long drawn out string of stars winding across the sky and terminating in the south with Achernar. Achernar can be seen only south of 33 degrees northern latitude and is thus a star primarily of the Southern Hemisphere. Achernar is about 88 light-years away from Earth and shines 650 times more brightly than the Sun. Its diameter is estimated to be seven times that of the Sun.

Algol

Algol is the second brightest star in the constellation Perseus and also the most famous variable star (see pages 150–51). Its brightness fluctuates so much that the change can be noticed even without binoculars. This unusual behavior seems to be reflected in the star's name, which is derived from the Arabic expression Al Ra's al Ghul, which means demon's head. But despite this apparent causal connection there is no indication that astronomers of ancient times, whether Greek, Roman, or Arab, were aware of the phenomenon of variable stars.

In old depictions of the constellation Perseus (see pages 30–31) Medusa's head is located where the demon star is. Algol consists of two stars that revolve around each other and alternately cover each other up (as in a solar eclipse) in a regular cycle, causing the light of Algol to dim.

Today we know that Algol is about 100 light-years distant from Earth and that its two stars

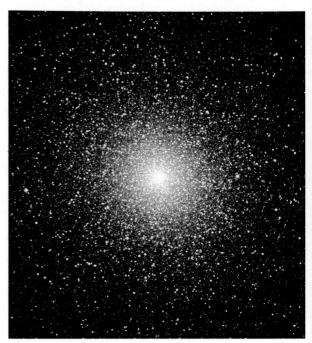

The globular star cluster 47 Tucanae.

revolve around each other in exactly 2 days, 20 hours, and 49 minutes. When the darker star moves in front of the brighter one, the luminosity of the binary declines by a factor of about 3 for 10 hours. This dimming is clearly visible. The brighter of the two stars is 100 times brighter than the Sun and has a diameter of 2.8 million miles (4.5 million km). It is thus one of the so-called supergiant stars. Very little is known about its darker companion star. Because it covers up the brighter star for such a long time span it must be even bigger, but at the same time it is considerably less bright and probably has less mass as well.

Alpha Centauri

This is the only one of the ten brightest stars that generally is referred to by its scientific designation—first introduced by Johann Bayer—rather than by a common name. In 1603, Bayer devised a system of assigning letters of the Greek alphabet to the stars, followed by the genitive form of the constellation's Latin name. The stars within a constellation are listed in order of apparent brightness. Alpha is the brightest star in a constellation, Beta the second brightest, Gamma the third brightest, and so on. Thus, Alpha Centauri is the brightest star in the constellation Centaurus (see pages 86–87). This unusual star also has proper names, such as Rigel Kentaurus, foot of the centaur, or Toliman, but they have never gained wide usage.

A-B

Today Alpha Centauri is one of the best known of all the stars because it is, along with its companions, our closest stellar neighbor. It is a mere 4.3 light-years away, which amounts to 25 trillion miles (43 trillion km), a distance light travels in 4 years and 4 months. Alpha Centauri is thus 275,000 times farther away from Earth than the Sun. The Scottish astronomer Thomas Henderson first measured the distance of this star in 1839 from the observatory in Cape Town. But 150 years earlier the missionary Richaud had realized when examining Alpha Centauri in India through a small telescope that this was a binary star. It has in the meantime become one of the best known and most closely observed double stars. We now know that the two stars (Alpha Centauri A and Alpha Centauri B) revolve around each other once every 80 years and that the distance that separates them fluctuates between 1 and 3.2 billion miles (1.6 and 5.2 billion km). Both stars have approximately the same mass as the Sun, and the brighter of the two, Alpha Centauri A, resembles the Sun closely in other respects as well.

In 1915, the astronomer Innes discovered another, fainter star in the immediate vicinity of Alpha Centauri, a small star that, when measured in greater detail turned out to be even a little closer to Earth. It is called Proxima Centauri, the closest one in Centaurus, and is exactly .065 light-years or 382 billion miles (615 billion km) closer to us than Alpha Centauri. Proxima Centauri can, of course, be seen only through very large telescopes. Measuring 43,000 miles (70,000 km) across, it is 2,000 times less luminous than the Sun. It has not been settled conclusively to this time whether Proxima Centauri is physically part of the binary Alpha Centauri and thus bound to the larger stars by gravity or whether it appears in the same line of vision only by chance.

Arcturus

The watcher of the bear, as its name translates, belongs to the constellation Boötes (the Herdsman). Arcturus is the brightest star in the northern half of the celestial sphere, and many people think that it was the first star to have been given a name. Arcturus is 34 light-years distant and thus in the immediate neighborhood of our solar system. Its luminosity is about 110 times greater than that of the Sun, and the hot gases of which it is composed are 3,000 times more rarefied than those of the Sun. Arcturus is a red giant, a type of star that has expanded to an extreme degree. It is "cool" (surface temperature: about 4,200° C), and its gases are more diffused than gases in an airless space on Earth, that is, in a vacuum. It is only because of the huge size of these stars that enough energy is emitted from their surfaces to make them visible in spite of their astronomical distances from Earth.

In autumn of 1933, Arcturus had a moment of "world" fame when its light, conducted to a photoelectric cell, opened the World's Fair in Chicago. The light ray activated a switch that turned on the floodlights on the fair grounds. Arcturus was chosen for this because its distance was then estimated to be 40 light-years. Consequently the light ray that triggered the ceremonious opening presumably would have been generated and sent from Arcturus in 1893, when the World's Fair had last been held in Chicago.

Betelgeuse

Orion, one of the most impressive constellations in the sky, is also the only one to include two of the sky's brightest stars, namely Rigel (see page 146) and Betelgeuse. The names of both stars refer directly to the figure of Orion, the Hunter (see pages 54–55). Betelgeuse is a much corrupted form of the Arabic phrase meaning armpit of the giant, for Betelgeuse is shown in old representations in one of Orion's shoulders.

Betelgeuse is easy to spot even without binoculars because of its reddish color. It is a type of star that is called red supergiant by astronomers on account of the truly astronomical dimensions that characterize these stars. Betelgeuse may be as much as 500 to 800 times bigger than the Sun, that is, 430 to 680 million miles (700 to 1,100 million km) in diameter. The considerable difference between these two numbers is not the result of an error in calculation. Betelgeuse is a variable star, and its luminosity undergoes irregular fluctuations. The reason for this is that the star's diameter keeps expanding and contracting. If Betelgeuse were located where the Sun is, it would, when fully contracted, extend as far as Mars's orbit; at greatest expansion it would reach as far as Jupiter. Betelgeuse is approximately 1,040 light-years away from us and is one of the largest stars known.

Binaries

Many "fixed" stars do not travel through space in solitude but have one or more companions. They form double, triple, and

B

multiple star systems, in which the individual partners are held together by mutual gravitational force.

Most binaries (or double stars) reveal their multiple structure only when viewed through binoculars or, more often, through a large telescope with high powers of magnification. Some double stars are so close to each other that their separate bodies cannot be detected at all by visual observation. But precise inspection of their spectrum—the different colors into which their light can be separated—will reveal their double nature. The spectrum changes in characteristic ways when a star moves toward or away from Earth. Stars whose double structure becomes apparent only through an analysis of the spectrum are called "spectroscopic" binaries in contrast to "visual" binaries, whose component stars can be seen with binoculars or a telescope.

Binaries are of great importance in astronomy because they offer the only way of determining the mass of stars with some accuracy. The movement of the stars around each other is subject to the laws of gravity, and the force of gravity depends on the mass of the individual stars and on their distance from each other. The orbital paths of the stars making up a binary, paths that are precisely defined, therefore indicate the effect exerted by the mass and consequently the mass of the two stars. However, plotting the orbital paths of binaries is difficult because the movement along the orbital path is generally very slow. Some binaries take as much as 100 years or more to complete one orbit. Spectroscopic binaries, on the other hand, revolve around each other in as little as 100 days.

The following binaries are marked in the star maps:
• **Mizar-Alcor** in Ursa Major. Anyone with good eyesight can detect these as two separate stars (see pages 32–33). However, it is still unclear whether they actually belong together, that is, whether they revolve around a common gravitational center. The distance between them is ¼ of a light-year, which amounts to 1.5 trillion miles (2.5 trillion km).

Mizar, the brighter of the two, is a visual binary—the first to have been recognized as such. The discovery goes back to 1650 when it was made by the Italian astronomer Riccioli. Mizar is also one of the most famous binaries. It is 88 light-years away. Unfortunately, a small telescope is required to see it as a double star. The two Mizar stars take several thousand years to revolve once around each other. Both of them are in turn double stars—spectroscopic binaries. They are the first of their kind to have been discovered. The American astronomer E. C. Pickering first described them in 1889.

The surface of the planet Mercury—a composite of photographs taken by the Mariner.

B–C

• **Albireo** in Cygnus. It often is called the most beautiful of all the binaries. Its double structure is visible through binoculars. The two stars are 410 light-years away and are two completely different colors; one is orange, the other, blue. The stars are 760 and 120 times more luminous than the Sun. The brighter one, which is named Albireo A, is in turn a double star, a spectroscopic binary.

• **Epsilon Lyrae** Like Mizar-Alcor, Epsilon Lyrae can be detected with the naked eye only by people with excellent eyesight. The two components also are referred to as Epsilon 1 and Epsilon 2. When examined through an average size telescope, the two stars turn out to be binaries themselves. The stars of Epsilon Lyrae 1 revolve around each other once in about 1,200 years, those of Epsilon Lyrae 2, in about 600 years. All four stars are of equal brightness and are 150 light-years away from Earth.

Canopus

Canopus, the second brightest star of the sky, belongs to the constellation Carina and is one of the few stars named after a human figure, though not a historical personage but rather a legendary figure from Greek mythology. Canopus was chief pilot of the Greek fleet under Menelaos's command and guided it on the way home after the fall of Troy. He reached the Egyptian coast, where he died. King Menelaos erected a mausoleum in the helmsman's honor and also named the brilliant star that stood just barely above the horizon in the south after him. From the modern point of view, the name could not have been better chosen. Of the ten brightest stars,

Canopus is the farthest away from the ecliptic. Spacecraft launched to explore the planets of our solar system therefore use it as a fixed navigational reference point in space by which to orient their flights. Small sensors are trained on Canopus and emit steering signals when it moves out of the sensors' field of vision. All the other bright stars are too close to the ecliptic, on whose plane spacecraft also travel, and the angles between them and Earth and the Sun—the other two points of reference in space— are too small and unreliable to serve as orientation aids.

On the other hand, the extreme southerly position of Canopus has prevented it from being observed much. All the data about it is therefore less definite than than about the other bright stars. Its distance from Earth is given variously at anywhere between 100 and 1,200 light-years. Probably the actual distance is somewhere around 250 light-years. It is quite certain that Canopus is a very large, brilliant star, about 1,400 times brighter than the Sun and 30 times its size. Like the Sun, it seems to be a solitary star; no evidence of a companion star thus far has been detected.

Capella

The She-Goat in Auriga, the Charioteer's shoulder (see pages 48–49), is the only one of the ten brightest stars that never sets for observers in the higher latitudes of the Northern Hemisphere and is thus circumpolar (see pages 9–10). Its distance from Earth is 41 light-years; its mass is three times that of the Sun, and its diameter is 16 times as large as the Sun's.

Capella is a spectroscopic binary (see pages 131–33). What

actually is seen when one looks at Capella is two stars that revolve around each other once every 104 days. The mass and diameter of Capella therefore refer to the brighter of the two stars. Capella also has two considerably smaller companions, classified as dwarfs, that can be seen through a telescope. Thus Capella is actually a quadruple star.

However, to date, observation of the four stars has not yet yielded a clear composite picture of this star complex. The invisible Capella twin in particular cannot be measured exactly, and Capella therefore remains partially shrouded in mystery.

Comets

Comets are one of the most striking phenomena in the sky. Large comets with their tails streaming behind them sometimes streak across the entire sky and occasionally can be seen even during daylight. Most comets are invisible to the unaided eye. Every year an average of 20 to 30 comets appear, but most of them can be seen only through a telescope.

Comets revolve around the Sun just as planets do, but they follow very elongated, elliptical orbital paths (see pages 16–17). The time it takes to complete one orbit around the Sun varies from a few years to millions of years. Comets are visible only during a very small segment of their journey, namely when they are in the immediate vicinity of the Sun. There the Sun's radiation heats them up, causing some of their material to stream out from the head and form a tail. This tail is made up partially of dust and partially of gases, which are made to glow by the sunlight. The formation of the tail is strongly influenced by the Sun,

133

which is shown by the fact that the tails of comets always point in the direction exactly opposite from the Sun.

Today comets are pictured as something resembling a dirty snowball. They are not solid bodies like the planets but instead are made up of frozen gases and dust particles lodged in the gases. In their frozen state, comets cannot be seen from Earth at all because they are too small— usually only about 6 miles (10 km) in diameter—and don't reflect enough sunlight. It is only the evaporation caused by the Sun's heat that makes them visible.

Only very few comets have been observed often enough thus far for their orbit and consequently their reappearance in the sky to be calculated. The most famous of these so-called periodic comets is Halley's Comet, which has been observed repeatedly as a brilliant object in the sky over the past 2,000 years. Halley's Comet takes 76 years to complete its orbit around the Sun and will not appear again until the year 2061. The great majority of comets, however, approach the Sun unexpectedly from the depths of the solar system, so that their appearances cannot be calculated ahead of time. Because in their approach to the Sun all comets lose some of their matter in the form of their tails, comets cannot exist indefinitely. The life expectancy of Halley's Comet, for example, is put at only about 200,000 years. The remains of comets continue to travel through space along the same paths and some give rise to meteor showers (see page 139).

Fixed Stars

In contrast to the planets (from the Greek word *planasthai*, wan-

derer) the stars seem to be motionless, or fixed to their spots on the celestial sphere. But it only looks that way because they are so very far away from us— distances that are measured in light-years (see Fixed Stars Are Not as Immobile as They Seem on page 10). In reality the fixed stars also move in the sky, but they do so at such a slow pace that their motion (called "proper" motion) becomes visually apparent only over thousands of years (see pages 10–11) and otherwise can be proven to exist only through precision measurements.

The fixed stars shine with their own light. They are suns like our Sun, that is, spheres of incandescent gases (called plasma by scientists). In the interior of these spheres, energy is produced through thermonuclear reactions. The number of suns in the universe is vast beyond guessing. The unaided eye can detect about 4,000 stars on a very clear night; a telescope reveals many millions in the region of the Milky Way alone (see page 140). The brightest of the stars form the familiar constellations in our night skies.

The stars are so very far removed from Earth that their distance is difficult to measure. Distances up to about 70 light-years can be established with relative accuracy by using a method similar to triangulation, which is used by surveyors. Greater stellar distances are determined indirectly. Because a star (like any other luminous body) appears fainter the farther away it is, scientists try to calculate a star's magnitude theoretically by applying methods based on physics. They then compare the results with the actual magnitude observed. However, this method is less accurate, and the distances given

by different astronomers vary considerably, diverging sometimes as much as 100 percent, especially for very remote stars.

One of the most fascinating areas of research in modern astronomy is the study of the life history of stars. Stars are formed from huge interstellar gas clouds (see pages 141–42), in whose interior gases and particles of matter gradually concentrate. A star is born when, at the core of this concentrated mass, energy is first produced through the conversion of hydrogen, the most prevalent element in space, into helium. The star then goes on to spend the main part of its life in a stable state, shining with a steady light.

But at some point all the hydrogen is used up and the star enters its next life stage. It tries to find alternate sources of energy by transforming the helium it has produced. But this is accomplished only with difficulty. The interior parts of the star contract while the outer ones expand. The star swells up in size and becomes a red giant. Eventually, when all sources of energy are exhausted, the star's life comes to an end. The star goes through a final, cataclysmic reaction and then either dies in a spectacular supernova explosion or simply ceases to emit light (see pages 149–50). The outer layers go hurling into space as gas nebulas, and what remains is either a star corpse whose glow gradually fades away—a white dwarf (see Sirius, pages 146–47)—or a neutron star. Conditions in such a neutron star are beyond anything imaginable: The mass of the entire Sun can be compressed into a ball 6 to 12 miles (10–20 km) in diameter, and one cubic centimeter of matter weighs 10 million to 1 billion tons! The life span of a star depends largely on its initial mass. Heavy stars with more than 5 times the mass of our Sun live for a relatively short time, about 100 to 200 million years, whereas stars like our Sun have a life span of 7 to 10 billion years.

Galaxies

The Milky Way, also called Our Galaxy, has provided the word used to refer to the islands of stars (galaxies) that exist in countless numbers (at least 3 billion) in the vastness of space. Each galaxy is a star system composed of stars, gases, and dust. Large galaxies, such as the Milky Way, contain several hundred billion stars. Smaller ones, such as the Small Magellanic Cloud, still have several hundred million stars.

The galaxies are removed from each other by unimaginable distances—at least hundreds of thousands or, more commonly, many million light-years. The vast regions of space that intervene between them are practically empty. Except for the Magellanic Clouds in the southern sky and the Andromeda Galaxy in the northern sky, galaxies can be seen only through telescopes.

The Andromeda Galaxy, about 2.2 million light-years away and in many ways similar to our own galaxy, the Milky Way, is one of the most familiar celestial objects. It appears to the naked eye as a blurred patch, but through a telescope one clearly can make out an elongated spindle of light. It and the Magellanic Clouds are among the Milky Way's closest neighbors. The galaxies thus far mentioned plus 30 dwarf galaxies all belong to a cluster of galaxies known as the Local Group, which extends across about 5 million

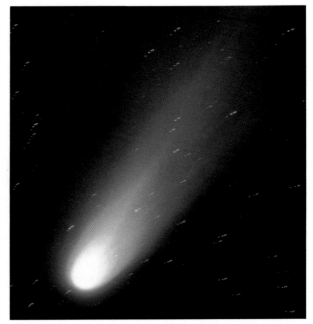

Halley's Comet during its last appearance close to Earth in 1986.

light-years. The Milky Way and the Andromeda Galaxy are the largest, most dominant members of the group. On the basis of their shape, galaxies are classified as being elliptical, spiral, barred spiral, and irregular. The most beautiful are the spiral shaped ones, of which the Andromeda Galaxy and the Milky Way are examples. In this type of galaxy, stars and gas clouds move around a large center with a great deal of mass, forming spiral-like arms the way a pinwheel does. The total number of stars in the Andromeda Galaxy is estimated at 400 billion and its diameter at about 100,000 light-years. In the past, this galaxy was referred to as the Andromeda Nebula; this name no longer is in use because the term nebula

is now reserved for masses of gas inside the Milky Way. The technical name for this celestial body is M 31, which stands for the fact that this is the 31st entry in the catalog of celestial objects compiled by Charles Messier (see photo, page 26).

The Hyades

The constellation Taurus includes not only the Pleiades (see page 145) but also a second open star cluster, the Hyades. This cluster is easily visible to the unaided eye as a V west of the star Aldebaran. The name Hyades comes from the Greek and means rainy stars. The Hyades rise at dusk in autumn (see star maps for October). In earlier times they were considered harbingers of the rainy season.

H–J

The Hyades are composed of about 350 stars and are situated 150 light-years away from Earth. This makes them the second closest open star cluster, and it is this relative closeness to us that lends special interest to them for astronomers. The Hyades have become a kind of milepost for measuring distances in the universe.

In the case of the Hyades, a method for determining distance can be employed that works especially well and yields exact values without depending on special assumptions. The measurement of 150 light-years thus obtained is then used to gauge the magnitude of some stars whose spectra display certain characteristic features. If these features are then found in other stars, the difference between the brightness of the stars within the Hyades and that of the stars under actual observation is used to calculate the distance of these other stars (all radiant objects appear fainter and fainter the farther away they are). Thus an error in the assumption of the Hyades's distance seriously would affect the distance calculations of galaxies (see page 135) millions of light-years away. New attempts keep being made to measure the distance of the Hyades, but thus far the estimate of 150 light-years has proven fairly accurate.

Jupiter

Jupiter is the largest planet of our solar system, larger and heavier than all the other planets taken together. Its name, the Roman version of Zeus who was the chief god and father of the Greek pantheon, does justice to Jupiter's position—the planet was dubbed the "royal star" by astronomers of antiquity.

The size of Jupiter is matched by the complexity of its system

The colorful atmosphere of the planet Jupiter.

of satellites. Sixteen satellites have been identified thus far, four of which (discovered in 1614 by Galileo Galilei) are quite large, large enough to be seen through binoculars. Jupiter's makeup differs completely from that of the planets Mercury, Venus, Earth, and Mars, all of which are closer to the Sun. Jupiter is made up primarily of hydrogen gas, helium, and methane. It is thus a mass of gases, presumably surrounding a massive and dense core. It has a very extensive, thick atmosphere that is shaken by huge storms whose power and ferocity hardly can be imagined here on Earth. On the surface of Jupiter, one can detect huge swirls of clouds that can last for hundreds of years and grow as large as 25,000 miles (40,000 km) across.

Knowledge of the largest planet was added to considerably in 1979 when the American Voyager space probes passed by it. The instruments on the craft observed not only the chaotic weather patterns on Jupiter but also the planet's large moons.

The moons turned out to be almost more interesting than Jupiter itself. This is true especially of Io, the closest of the satellites, on whose surface the first active volcanoes in the solar system were discovered (discounting the ones on Earth). Another advance in our knowledge about Jupiter is expected when the spacecraft Galileo is expected to reach the giant planet in December of 1995 after a six-year journey.

Basic Data of Jupiter

Distance to the Sun:	484 million miles (779 million km)
Period of revolution about the Sun:	11.9 years
Diameter:	88,673 miles (142,790 km)
Period of rotation:	9 hours, 55 minutes
Mass:	318 times that of Earth

M

The Magellanic Clouds

Out of a total of at least 3 billion galaxies in the universe, only three can be seen with the naked eye. They are the Andromeda Galaxy, M 31, in the northern sky and the two Magellanic Clouds in the southern sky. Whereas the Andromeda Galaxy (see page 135) appears as nothing more than a small, fuzzy blob in the autumn sky, the two Magellanic Clouds can be seen distinctly any night of the year from any point south of 20 degrees south latitude. They are near enough to the south celestial pole to be circumpolar in that area (see North Pole, South Pole, and Equator on page 9).

Both Magellanic Clouds, which look almost like pieces that had broken off the Milky Way, are about 160,000 light-years distant and are thus the closest galaxies to our own, the Milky Way. Together with the Andromeda Galaxy, the Milky Way, and a few other smaller galaxies, they form a kind of "galaxy cluster" that moves through space together, the so-called Local Group. Astronomers count the two Clouds among the irregular dwarf galaxies. But this has to be understood as an astronomer's term, for the Greater Magellanic Cloud contains about 6 billion times—and the Lesser one about 1.5 billion times—the mass of the Sun in the form of innumerable stars as well as gas and dust nebulas (see photos, pages 78 and 152–53). The two Magellanic Clouds form a stunning sight when viewed through binoculars. At observatories on the southern half of the globe they are *the* object of observation, and their study already has helped solve many astronomical problems. In January 1987, a supernova flared up in the Great Magellanic Cloud; it was the first supernova to be visible to the naked eye since the year 1604 (see pages 149–50).

Mars

Mars owes its name to its reddish color. It was named after the Roman god of war. The reddish color is due to Mars's extensive deserts covered with red sand.

In many respects, Mars resembles Earth. It has seasons like those of Earth, and it rotates around its axis in about the same amount of time as Earth does. It has a thin atmosphere, which is sometimes disturbed by quite violent weather with huge sand storms sometimes blocking the view of as much as half the planet's surface. Mars's polar caps, again like Earth's, are white, though most of the ice melts during the Mars summer. Because of these similarities to Earth it was thought in the last century that Mars might be inhabited, and to this day stories are being published in which Martians figure prominently.

Modern space exploration has, however, put an end to the belief that Mars might be inhabited. The only other planet that has been approached by space probes and vehicles as often as Mars is Venus. The culmination of the efforts to explore Mars came in 1976 when Viking I and Viking II landed on Mars and spent many months taking pictures of the planet's surface and picking up soil samples (see photo, page 139). The findings give no indication whatsoever of the existence of any form of life on Mars, no matter how primitive. The photographs show Mars to be covered with a great many craters and also with strange rills that look like rivers. It seems as if there had once been water on the surface of Mars many millions of years ago.

Mars, which is only half the size of Earth, can be observed only with difficulty. All that can be seen through a telescope at high magnification are light and dark areas. They were all that cartographers had to go on to construct maps of Mars before the age of space exploration.

Basic Data of Mars

Distance to the Sun:	142 million miles (227.9 million km)
Period of revolution about the Sun:	687 days
Diameter:	4,220 miles (6,794 km)
Period of rotation:	24 hours, 37 minutes
Mass:	.11 times that of Earth

Mercury

The winged messenger of the Greek gods lent his name to the planet closest to the Sun. The people of antiquity had already noticed that of all the planets Mercury moves across the sky with the greatest speed. It can be seen only for about a week at a time in the evening dusk or for about a week in the morning dawn, low in the horizon (see table, pages 114–15).

Mercury's speed is due entirely to its proximity to the Sun. Of the nine major planets of the solar system, Mercury is the one nearest to the Sun. Because the Sun's gravitational pull is especially strong there, Mercury has to move fast in order not to be

M

drawn off its course and plunge toward the Sun. The great closeness to the Sun also affects the planet's surface drastically. On the side turned toward the Sun the temperature can rise to 400° C, whereas on the side facing away it drops below minus 200° C. The temperature difference is so extreme because Mercury has no atmosphere like Earth's that could act as a buffer.

Thus far only one space probe has approached Mercury. This was Mariner 10, which passed very close to Mercury three times in the years 1974 and 1975, as close as 203 miles (327 km) at the last flyby on March 16, 1975. The cameras transmitted thousands of sharp television pictures to Earth, which show the planet's surface to be a stony desert pockmarked by craters. Mercury looks very similar to the Moon. On the basis of the photographs taken by Mariner 10, detailed maps of Mercury have been made on which many craters are named after astronomers and other famous personages. Some of Mercury's craters are extremely large; thus the crater Beethoven

measures 388 miles (625 km) across. But there are also large, smooth plains on the planet, such as the Calores Basin, which extends across about 800 miles (1,300 km). Presumably the Mercury craters were caused, like those of the Moon, by the impact of large meteorites (see pages 138–39) many million or even billion years ago.

Basic Data of Mercury

Distance to the Sun:	36 million miles (57.9 million km)
Period of revolution about the Sun:	88 days
Diameter:	3,029 miles (4,878 km)
Period of rotation:	58 days
Mass:	.05 times that of Earth

Meteors and Meteorites

On a clear night, one frequently sees brief streaks of light in the sky—the shooting stars or meteors. Their sometimes striking trails that shoot across the sky at lightning speed are caused by tiny particles of dust, often the remains of comets, penetrating into Earth's atmosphere.

The air that is set ablaze as a meteor enters the atmosphere appears to us as the trail of a shooting star. Even a grain of dust less than one gram in weight can cause a meteor that looks brighter than the brightest stars.

Most shooting stars light up for only a fraction of a second. But there are also some, called fireballs, that are extremely bright and even produce sound. When the piece of matter that enters Earth's atmosphere from outer space is quite large, it may not be completely incinerated in its passage through the air but may survive and fall to Earth. These fragments from outer space are called meteorites. Unfortunately it is impossible to predict the arrival of meteorites or the appearance of meteors. Their occurrence is a matter of pure chance, although there are two interesting general patterns.

One is that meteors are always more numerous in the morning than in the evening, by

Meteor Showers

Name	Period of Visibility	Maximum	Number of Meteors per hour	Origin
Quarantids (Boötes)	1/1–1/4	1/3	40	unknown
Lyrids	4/12–4/24	4/22	15	Comet 1861 I
May Aquarids	4/28–5/21	5/5	20	Halley's Comet
July Aquarids	7/25–8/10	7/29	20	unknown
Perseids	7/20–8/19	8/11	50	Comet 1862 III
Orionids	10/11–10/30	10/20	25	Halley's Comet
Leonids	11/14–11/20	11/17	15 (variable in 1966 over 100,000!)	Comet 1866 I
Geminids	12/5–12/19	12/12	50	Asteroid Phaeton?

M

Olympus Mons, the largest volcano on Mars, photographed by Viking I.

roughly a factor of four. This is because in the morning we face in the direction of Earth's movement. Consequently our planet, racing along its orbit around the Sun, literally sweeps up more dust from space than it does in the evening when we look out in the direction opposite to Earth's movement, watching, so to speak, the wake of Earth's progress. The second predictable factor is that there are certain times of the year when more meteors than ordinary are produced—what are called meteor showers.

Meteor Showers

When comets disintegrate (see page 133) and dissipate their dust particles into space, these particles continue to orbit along the comet's path around the Sun. Every time Earth cuts across such a dense trail of dust, an unusually large number of particles enters Earth's atmosphere, causing many meteors to appear.

These are the meteor showers or swarms.

Just as it looks to us, when we drive along a highway, as though the trees along the side of the road were flying toward us from a distant point ahead and whizzing past the car's side, so the meteors of a swarm seem to emanate from one spot in the sky and scatter from there in all directions. The name of the constellation from which a given meteor shower seems to originate is used in that shower's designation.

At the present time, the Perseids are the most prolific meteor showers. Because they are most plentiful in August, on the day of St. Lawrence, they are also called the Tears of Saint Lawrence. The Quadrantids, which appear in early January in the area of Boötes, are named for Quadrans (the Quadrant), an ancient constellation that is no longer recognized.

The most interesting meteor showers are the Leonids. They

appear annually, but once every 33 years Earth traverses an especially heavy concentration of dust particles, and then meteors show up in such amazing numbers that the whole sky appears lit up. This happened on November 12, 1799 (observed by Alexander von Humboldt in South America), on November 12, 1833, and again on November 14, 1866, when 7,200 shooting stars per hour were observed. But in 1899 the Leonids failed to appear, and they were not seen again until November 14, 1966, when the most massive shower of meteors of all time was witnessed in the American Midwest, with at times as many as 40 meteors per second (a rate that translates into 144,000 per hour!). How the Leonids will behave in the future is hard to predict, but there are projections suggesting heightened activity in November of the years 1997–1999, with November 17, 1998 as the most likely date.

M

The center of the Milky Way—an aggregation of innumerable stars.

The Milky Way

One of the most striking celestial objects is the band of light, irregular in outline and broken up in places by dark areas, that arches across the sky. The Milky Way's band of muted luminosity fascinated the ancient astronomers and has given rise to the most diverse mythological explanations (see pages 40–41 and 48–49). The best known of these old legends still provides the basis for the modern technical name for the Milky Way, namely, the Galaxy (*gala* is the Greek word for milk).

The Galaxy, or Milky Way, is the cosmic home of our Sun and Earth in the universe. It is a huge system of stars in the shape of a disk. Regarded from a point outside of it, the Milky Way would look much like the Andromeda Galaxy, which is a sister galaxy of the Milky Way (see page 135). It has a diameter of 100,000 light-years. Millions of stars revolve in huge orbits around an immense central section that must contain a mass at

least 70 million larger than our Sun. For reasons not yet understood, the stars are arranged in spiral arms. Looked at from above, the Galaxy therefore would look like a pinwheel of astronomical proportions. Our solar system is located in the outer reaches of the Galaxy, about 28,000 light-years from the center. At this distance, our solar system takes about 200 million years to circle once around the Galaxy's center. The spiral arms of the Milky Way Galaxy move around this center similarly to the way Earth and the other planets revolve around the Sun.

The stars are largely concentrated along the plane of the Milky Way's disk, and because Earth also lies on this plane, our Galaxy's stars seem to be arranged in a band around Earth. We are able to see only the closest ones individually; the millions of stars in the Galaxy's spiral arms blur together to form a luminous area. Because there are also many gas and dust clouds

located in the spiral arms, this band appears jagged and in places seems to have holes and fissures. Some examples of this are the Coalsack in the constellation of the Southern Cross (see pages 84–85) and the area of the constellation Cygnus, where the Milky Way seems to divide in two separate strands (see pages 44–45).

The band of the Milky Way is so faint that excellent viewing conditions are required for its observation. Preferably the night should not be moonlit.

Mira

The Wonderful Star (*mira* is the Latin word for wonderful) is part of the constellation Cetus and was the first variable star to be discovered (see pages 74–75). It was first observed as early as 1596 by the East Frisian pastor David Fabricius, who assumed he had discovered a new star but then could not find it again until 1606 and therefore named it Mira. It was not realized until 1638 that this was a variable star that at the peak of its luminosity is easily visible to the naked eye but can be discerned only with the aid of a telescope in its faintest phase. Mira, which is 220 light-years away from Earth, belongs to the class of red giants. Its brightness fluctuates regularly in periods of about 330 days or approximately 11 months. Mira is a pulsating star; that is, it alternately expands and contracts, thus changing the size of its light-radiating surface. At maximum brightness, Mira is about 500 times the size of our Sun; at minimum brightness, about 350 times. Today a total of about 5,000 stars are known that fluctuate in magnitude for the same reasons and therefore are called Mira-type variables.

The Moon

Most of the planets in our solar system are accompanied by satellites or moons. The word moon used in this sense obviously derives from our Moon, Earth's traveling companion.

Earth has only one satellite, but it occupies a special place in the solar system because it is one of the largest satellites when regarded in terms of the size of the bodies around which they orbit. The Moon's mass is about ⅛₁ that of Earth, whereas the satellites of the other planets (except for Pluto) have less than ⅟₁₀₀₀ of the mass of the planet they circle. For this reason it is easier to think of Earth and the Moon as a kind of double planet traveling around the Sun together.

The Moon is the closest heavenly object to Earth and the only one, apart from the Sun, that appears as a disk to the naked-eye observer. One clearly can make out dark and light spots on its surface that add up to something that can be interpreted to look

like a face (the "man in the moon"). The dark spots are low-lying areas on the Moon's surface that are covered with dark lava. These are called the Moon's seas or maria and have very few craters. The light areas indicate areas of greater altitude that are covered with granite-like rocks and dotted with a multitude of craters. They are sometimes called the Moon's continents even though there is no water on the Moon. These names go back to the time of the first examinations of the Moon through telescopes.

Even a look through binoculars reveals how densely some of the Moon's surface is covered with craters. One also can see mountain ranges, such as the Lunar Apennines and the Lunar Alps. The Moon's craters, some of which can measure as much as 125 miles (200 km) across, are named after great scientists and other famous persons in world history. The names of the Moon's seas are more imaginative. The Moon's appearance varies as its position in relation to Earth and the Sun changes. These moon phases (for details on how they are produced, see pages 105–07) also affect significantly what is seen when observing the Moon through binoculars. At full moon, the moon craters and mountains do not cast any shadows, so that they do not stand out three-dimensionally. The craters, mountains, and maria are easiest to see in the border area between the light and dark sides of the Moon. Look for them in the evening and preferably during the first quarter phase (see Table of Lunar Phases, pages 106–07).

The same side of the Moon always is visible because the Moon takes the same amount of

time to rotate around its axis and to revolve around Earth. But now, thanks to photographs taken by many spacecraft circling the Moon, it is known exactly what its far side looks like. To date, 12 astronauts aboard six spacecraft, the American Apollo missions 11 to 17, have landed on the Moon, as have about two dozen unmanned space vehicles. The Moon therefore is the most thoroughly explored celestial object.

Basic Data of the Moon

Average distance from Earth:	239,000 miles (384,400 km)
Period of revolution around Earth:	27⅓ days (sidereal month; that is, one orbit relative to a fixed point, such as a distant star)
	29½ days (synodic month; that is, one cycle from new moon to new moon as seen from Earth)
Diameter:	2,160 miles (3,476 km) (.27 times Earth's diameter)
Mass:	⅛₁ of Earth's mass

Nebulas

The space between the stars is not a void. It is filled with so-called interstellar material; however, the density of this material is so extremely low that the emptiest vacuum that can be created on Earth would seem like a packed hall by comparison. In one liter capacity of interstellar space there are at most 50,000 to

100,000 atoms, whereas the same unit of capacity filled with Earth's air contains 30 sextillion atoms (that is a 3 followed by 22 zeroes!).

Ninety-nine percent of the interstellar material is made up of gases—hydrogen and helium atoms—the other one percent consists of dust particles. Together they form the cosmic nebulas, which are some of the loveliest and most colorful phenomena in space. When there are bright stars in the vicinity of a gaseous nebula, the energy-rich ultraviolet light from the stars causes the gases to emit light of their own. The gases then glow in various colors and sometimes chaotic shapes, whereas the dust clouds project the most fantastic silhouettes against these brilliant walls of light. The dust clouds intercept and absorb the light rays that are on their way toward Earth.

Viewed without optical magnification, the cosmic nebulas appear only as small, fuzzy patches, but their striking shapes can be glimpsed even through binoculars and are, of course, much more impressive when seen through a telescope. The colors show up only on photographs taken with huge telescopes and long exposure times. The three most famous nebulas, which are marked in the star charts, are:

• **The Great Nebula in Orion or M 42** This is the brightest nebula in the sky and is considered by many astronomers to be the greatest celestial showpiece. With a diameter of 100,000 light-years it covers a sizable piece of the sky. To many viewers who glimpse it through a telescope, it seems like chaos in visible form. M 42 is 1,500 light-years distant from us and owes its great luminosity to four extremely bright stars at its center. These stars are known as the Trapezium in Orion because they seem to form the corners of this geometrical figure (see photo, page 52).

• **The Lagoon Nebula or M 8** The English astronomer John Flamsteed discovered this galactic nebula in the constellation Sagittarius in the year 1747. It shines forth among the stars of the Milky Way with an intensive red, the color emitted by hydrogen gas at a temperature of about 10,000 degrees. A dark cloud cuts across this brightly shining mass of gas and creates the impression of a lagoon (see photo, page 5). There is enough gas in the Lagoon Nebula to form 200 suns. The nebula is about 3,000 light-years away.

• **Eta Carinae Nebula** This is one of the most beautiful objects in the southern region of the Milky Way. A huge hydrogen cloud surrounds the star Eta Carinae at a distance from Earth of about 6,000 light-years. It is to this star of superlatives, which was for a long time taken to be the brightest and heaviest star of the entire Milky Way Galaxy, that the nebula owes its luminosity. This is because Eta Carinae radiates at least 4 million times more light than the Sun and thus excites the gas atoms within a radius of several light-years to light up.

Today Eta Carinae, the star that gave rise to the nebula, is no longer visible to the naked eye. But during the last century, it was among the brightest stars in the sky. In 1843, it was the second brightest, right after Sirius, but after that its magnitude declined rapidly until, by 1865, it had become an object visible only through a telescope, and it has remained more or less unchanged since then. The reason for this strange change is still a mystery today. The most recent measurements seem to indicate that Eta Carinae is actually a multiple star consisting of four or five stars, and many astronomers see in it a possible candidate for the next supernova explosion in the Milky Way sometime within the next hundred years (see pages 149–50).

Northern and Southern Lights

In the high latitudes both north and south, around the magnetic poles, one often can observe amazing light shows in the sky at night. Ghostlike greenish and reddish beams of light and entire walls of light chase across the sky or may hover overhead for hours without moving. These auroras, or northern and southern lights, are caused by the Sun, which emits a steady stream of charged particles into space. Earth's magnetic field directs these particles toward the polar regions, where they collide with molecules in the air and excite them to glow. Northern (and southern) lights are especially frequent at the peak of sunspot cycles.

Novas

From time to time stars blaze up unexpectedly in the sky and become so bright that they are visible to the unaided eye for a few days or weeks before sinking into obscurity again. They undergo such a sudden and dramatic increase in magnitude that they might be taken for new stars (*nova* is Latin for new). In fact they exist both before and after their spectacular performance. Novas are variable stars (see pages 150–51) whose fluctuations in magnitude do not follow a more or less regular pattern but happen abruptly and are some-

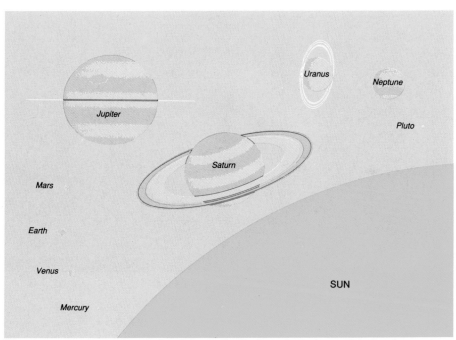

The planets vary in size, but the Sun (whose edge is shown in the lower right-hand corner) dwarfs them all.

times of stupendous dimensions. For example, in the year 1975 the nova in the constellation Cygnus increased in magnitude by a factor of 40 million within a few days (see pages 44–45). Then, over a period of several weeks, it gradually returned to its previous level. There are also stars in which nova explosions have been observed more than once.

Astronomers suspect today that all novas are binaries (see page 131). One of the two stars is a very small, hot, and dense white dwarf (see pages 146–47); the other, a large, cool, reddish star. The two are so close to each other that matter keeps being drawn from the larger to the smaller one. Eventually so much matter from the larger companion accumulates on the surface

of the white dwarf that it begins to ignite spontaneously. Hydrogen fuses into helium by means of the same process that goes on in the interior of stars, including our Sun (see page 149). But here the nuclear fusion is not controlled as it is in the Sun but instead takes the form of an explosion—similar to the explosion of hydrogen bombs here on Earth, which function on the same principle of fusing hydrogen into helium. During the gigantic explosion of a nova, the hot hydrogen layer enveloping the small star is shed, and the whole game can start over until the larger star has lost all its outer matter to the smaller one.

Novas are to be distinguished from supernovas (see pages 149–50).

The Planets

The planets of our solar system appear in our sky as nothing more than dots of light just like the fixed stars (see pages 133–34). Yet the difference between these two groups of heavenly objects could hardly be greater. Planets are cold celestial bodies that revolve around the Sun and are illuminated by it. They are much closer to Earth than any stars, their distance ranging from 24 million miles or 38.3 million km (Venus at its closest) to 4.6 billion miles or 7.5 billion km (Pluto at its farthest). The closest star to us, Alpha Centauri (see pages 130–31), is about 27 trillion miles (43 trillion km) away.

Astronomers suspect today that many stars have planetary systems. However, despite many

P

The planet Saturn in a photograph taken by Voyager I with colors added by computer.

tries, no one has been able thus far to supply conclusive proof that this is so. We therefore know only one planetary system at this point, namely that of the Sun. It consists of nine major planets and a large, indeterminate number of minor planets or asteroids. These minor planets can be seen only through a telescope and, because of their small size, show up even there only as tiny dots, like stars. Most of them orbit around the Sun between Mars and Jupiter. Today the paths of about 4,000 asteroids, almost all of which have been given names, are known. In earlier times they were named after legendary figures, now mostly after astronomers and other natural scientists.

By contrast, clear details can be observed in the surface of the major planets when they are examined through a telescope. Still, exact knowledge of the planets had to wait until the age of space exploration, when space probes photographed and measured the planets from up close and transmitted the data back to Earth. At this point in time, all the major planets have been visited by space probes with the exception of Pluto, which is farthest away from the Sun. The most sensational accomplishments were scored by Voyager II, which started out in 1977 and traveled until 1989, making an almost incredible journey of 3.7 billion miles (6 billion km) through the solar system, in the course of which it reached Jupiter, Saturn, Uranus, and Neptune.

Three of the major planets cannot be seen with the naked eye but are nevertheless also very interesting. They are:

• **Uranus** It was discovered in

Basic Data of the Planets	Uranus	Neptune	Pluto
Distance from the Sun:	1.7 billion miles (2.8 billion km)	2.8 billion miles (4.5 billion km)	3.7 billion miles (5.9 billion km)
Period of revolution about the Sun:	84.6 years	165.5 years	248 years
Diameter:	31,500 miles (50,800 km)	30,200 miles (48,600 km)	1,860 miles (3,000 km)
Mass:	14 times that of Earth	17 times that of Earth	.002 times that of Earth

P

1781 by the German-English astronomer William Herschel. Uranus greatly resembles Jupiter in physical structure, consisting primarily of gases, but its mass is considerably less. In pictures taken by Voyager II on a flyby in 1986, Uranus revealed itself as a quiet planet with surprisingly few notable features in its dense atmosphere, which shimmers in a bluish color.

• **Neptune** The discovery of Neptune in 1846 was one of the greatest triumphs of natural science in the nineteenth century. The English astronomer J. C. Adams and the French astronomer U. C. Leverrier independently from each other had predicted the existence of the planet. Both had observed that Uranus did not orbit around the Sun along the path it should have followed according to astronomical calculations. They consequently theorized that the gravitational force of another planet must be acting on Uranus, causing it to deviate from its path, and, basing their calculations on the observed deviations, they predicted the location of the missing planet. Neptune was found exactly where the scientists had said it would be.

Very little was known about this planet before August 1989 when Voyager II reached it. To everyone's surprise, the space probe's photographs showed Neptune to be a very active planet—far more active than Uranus—with a great deal of turbulence and large bands of clouds in its atmosphere. Neptune, like Uranus, resembles Jupiter in consisting primarily of gases.

• **Pluto** The American Clyde Tombaugh spotted Pluto in 1930. But it was not until 1978 that a moon, Charon, was discovered orbiting around Pluto. From this satellite's path astronomers were able to calculate the mass and estimate the diameter of Pluto (see Binaries, page 131). Pluto turned out to be by far the smallest and lightest planet of the solar system. Many astronomers suspect that Pluto might once have been a moon of Neptune.

The Pleiades

The seven daughters of the giant Atlas (see pages 54–55) not only turned Orion's head with their beauty but also were transformed by the gods into one of the most beautiful objects in the sky. On a clear winter night, they are visible in the constellation Taurus as a faintly shimmering patch that looks very impressive when viewed through binoculars. The unaided eye can make out from six to thirteen stars, seven of which bear the names of the seven sisters: Alcyone (the brightest of the stars), Maia, Asterope, Tageta, Celaeno, Electra, and Merope. The Pleiades are the most well-known open star cluster (see pages 148–49). This cluster is made up of about 130 stars spread out over an area of 30 light-years. The Pleiades are 410 light-years away from Earth and are one of the younger star clusters. They are thought to be about 60 million years old.

The stars of the Pleiades are enveloped by wisps of tenuous nebulas that can be seen clearly in photographs taken with long exposure times. These nebulas are dust clouds that reflect the light of the stars constituting the Pleiades (see photo, page 147).

The Praesepe

The Praesepe, also called the Beehive, is another open star cluster in addition to the Pleiades and the Hyades (see page 135) that has a descriptive name (*praesepe* is Latin for manger). This star cluster is located in the constellation Cancer. Its technical name, which is the one used in the star maps, is M 44. Viewed through binoculars, the Praesepe is the second most impressive open star cluster after the Pleiades.

A total of about 500 stars are contained in the Praesepe, which is 520 light-years away from Earth. They are distributed over a space of 15 light-years and are approximately 400 million years old (see photo, page 25).

Procyon

Stars appear especially bright in our sky for one of two reasons: They are either exceptionally large and produce immense quantities of energy, as in the case of Betelgeuse (see page 131) and Rigel (see page 146), or they are very close to Earth, like Alpha Centauri (see pages 130–31) and Sirius (see pages 146–47).

Procyon in the constellation Canis Minor belongs to the second group. Without Procyon, this small constellation would hardly be worth mentioning. The name Procyon comes from the Greek and means before the dog. The reason for the name is that Procyon appears in the east shortly before its more striking companion, Sirius in Canis Major. Procyon is a star similar to our Sun, but about six times brighter and twice its size. Astronomers were able to determine its mass more precisely than that of Sirius because Procyon is a binary (see page 131). Its partner revolves around it in 40 years and is a white dwarf. In this respect, too, Procyon resembles its big brother, Sirius. The mass of Procyon has been estimated at 1.7 times that of the Sun; that of its much smaller companion star, at .65 the mass of our Sun.

R–S

Rigel

Rijel Jauzah al Yusra (the left leg of the giant) is what Arabian astronomers called the bright white star in Orion (see pages 54–55). This name survives today in the much abbreviated form Rigel. Rigel is a star of truly astronomical dimensions. Of the ten stars that appear brightest in the sky, it is the one farthest removed from Earth; astronomers estimate the distance variously from 900 to 1,300 light-years. The fact that Rigel is nevertheless so prominent in our sky means that it must generate immense amounts of energy. Astronomers class it as a supergiant, with a surface temperature of 12,000 degrees and an absolute magnitude equal to that of 57,000 suns. Other basic data about it includes a mass 30 times that of the Sun and a diameter 19 times greater. It shines 40 times brighter than Venus and is almost a fifth as bright as the Moon at full moon.

Saturn

The most beautiful of the Sun's planets is no doubt Saturn. Although it is known now, thanks to the flybys of the great space probes, that Jupiter, Uranus, and Neptune also have rings, Saturn's are by far the biggest. Even through a small telescope—though not binoculars—Saturn's highly impressive ring system is visible at a magnification of 40 or above.

Saturn is encircled by several rings. These are not solid but are made up of huge numbers of dust particles and small, gravel-like rocks that orbit around the planet. It is the great distance from Earth that fuses these countless pieces of material into an image of solid rings. The pictures taken by Voyager I and Voyager II, which passed by Saturn in November 1980 and August 1981, show the exact composition of the planet's ring system. The rings are thought to be the remains of a Saturnian moon that approached the mother planet too closely millions of years ago and was torn asunder by it. Saturn has other moons, some of which were not known until the space probes revealed them. One of these satellites, appropriately named Titan, vies with Jupiter's moon Ganymede for the rank of the largest planetary companion in the solar system. It, too, can be seen from Earth—with the aid of binoculars—and has a diameter of 3,240 miles (5,220 km).

Like Jupiter, Saturn consists of very light gases, primarily hydrogen, methane, and ammonia. The density of its material is so light that the planet would float on water. By contrast, Earth, which, like Mars and Venus, consists of metals and heavy minerals, would immediately sink to the bottom in such an imaginary experiment. Again as in the case of Jupiter, the outer surface of Saturn's atmosphere moves and shows bands of clouds and huge disturbances. But these atmospheric activities clearly are minor when compared to the tremendous storms that take place on Jupiter.

Astronomers hope to obtain more detailed information about Saturn primarily from the flight of Cassini, a space probe scheduled to be launched toward Saturn in 1995. This spacecraft is scheduled to reach the vicinity of the distant planet in the fall of 2002 and then veer toward it. It will release a small module with scientific instruments that will parachute toward and land on Saturn's moon Titan.

Basic Data of Saturn

Distance to the Sun:	890 million miles (1,432 million km)
Period of revolution about the Sun:	29.6 years
Diameter:	74,500 miles (120,000 km)
Period of rotation:	10 hours, 40 minutes
Mass:	95 times that of Earth

Sirius

Sirius, the most famous of the stars, owes its great apparent magnitude primarily to the simple fact that it is only 8.7 light-years away from Earth. It sends out 23 times as much light as the Sun and is 1.8 times larger than it. Compared to stars like Rigel or Betelgeuse (see page 131), Sirius is relatively small. But the history of the brightest star is unusual and remarkable. In ancient Egypt, Sirius enjoyed godlike veneration because its appearance in the sky heralded the flooding of the Nile (see pages 56–57), and in ancient Rome, dogs were sacrificed to it. Astronomers in those early times consistently described Sirius as being reddish, indeed, redder than the planet Mars. Today its light is pure white, as a glance into the sky will show.

How can a star change its color over a period of barely 1,500 years? This question has found no convincing answer to this day. It is one of the great riddles of stellar astronomy, the study of fixed stars. For although stars do pass through different stages of development, such unmistakable, clearly visible

S

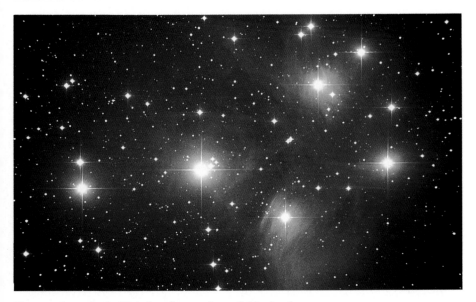

The star cluster in the Pleiades, the most beautiful in the sky.

changes as a shift of color from red to white require, according to all accepted theories, several hundred thousand years to complete, not a mere one and a half millenia.

Perhaps Sirius's mysterious change of color has something to do with its companion, for Sirius is a binary. As early as 1844, the German astronomer Friedrich Bessel had noted that Sirius does not move across the sky in a straight line (fixed stars do move, see page 134) but follows a serpentine path instead. Bessel concluded from this that Sirius must have an invisible companion whose gravity affects the behavior of its large partner. It took until 1862 before this companion, now officially named Sirius B, actually was discovered through a telescope as a very faint dot of light next to brightly shining Sirius A.

The actual discovery of Sirius B, or the Pup, as it is also known, presented a puzzle to astronomers. For on the basis of the two stars' movements (see Binaries, page 131–132) they had calculated that Sirius A must be 2.36 times as heavy and Sirius B .98 as heavy as the Sun. Because, however, Sirius B appeared so much fainter than its big brother (although its surface is extremely hot), it had to be much smaller, only about 18,000 miles (30,000 km) or about twice Earth's diameter. Such a large amount of matter concentrated in so little space meant a density that was beyond what anyone could imagine. One cubic centimeter of the matter making up Sirius B would weigh over 300 pounds (150 kg)! Thus Sirius B became the first example of a new type of star to be discovered, the white dwarfs. The characteristics of white dwarfs are extremely small size (the smallest one known thus far

is only half as big as the Moon), high surface temperature, and incredible concentration of the matter composing them. Astronomers say that the matter in a white dwarf has degenerated. White dwarfs are dying stars that no longer generate light and therefore gradually fade. They are the remains of stars whose "hearts," that is, the generation of energy inside them, have stopped. One might say that they are star corpses.

Star Clusters

Stars do not exist in the universe in random isolation. Instead they are organized in systems or galaxies within which, under the force of gravity, they revolve around each other or move along common paths. Thus all the visible stars are part of the Milky Way Galaxy (see page 140), and many of them have companions and are thus double or multiple

S

The planet Venus, photographed by the space probe Pioneer-Venus, looks sickle-shaped when on the same side of the Sun as Earth.

star systems (see page 131–132), or they form aggregations that include several dozen to many hundred stars, the star clusters. Our Sun, which is neither a member of a star cluster nor part of a multiple star system, is something of an exception in the Milky Way.

To date, astronomers have discovered about 1,000 star clusters in the Milky Way Galaxy alone. Depending on their appearance they are classified as either open star clusters, in which the stars are still individually recognizable in spite of their large number, or as globular star clusters, in which the stars are packed so close together that they appear as single white patches.

The three most famous star clusters are the Pleiades and the Hyades in the constellation Taurus (see pages 145 and 135) and the Praesepe, or the Beehive, in Cancer (see page 145). Apart from these, the following can be seen with the naked eye:

• **H and χ (chi) Persei** The constellation Perseus boasts not just one but two star clusters that are right next to each other and can be seen together through binoculars. Because they look almost like two stars to the naked eye, they have typical star names (see the Constellations and the Zodiac, starting on page 8). H Persei is somewhat more spectacular, having brighter stars. Both clusters are 8,000 light-years away from us, and they each contain 300 to 350 stars.

• **IC 2602 in Carina** The stars of this cluster also are referred to as the southern Pleiades. Their prosaic technical name indicates that they are the 2602nd entry in the Index Catalogue, a compilation of star clusters and nebulas. At a distance of 700 light-years, they are very close to Earth in astronomical terms. This cluster includes one especially bright star, Theta Carinae, with whose help it is easy to spot the cluster.

• **M 7 in Scorpius** is also an open star cluster. It is situated in a particularly starry region of the sky and therefore appears to the naked-eye observer as nothing more than a small, fuzzy patch in front of the luminous band of the Milky Way. M 7 is an aggregation of about 60 stars about 780 light-years away. This cluster was studied closely by the astronomer Charles Messier in the spring of 1746 and included as the seventh and the most southerly object in his catalog.

• **Omega Centauri** is the brightest of all the globular star clusters. The fact that in spite of a distance of 15,000 light-years this cluster can be recognized quite clearly as a star-like, fuzzy spot is an indication of its great inherent luminosity. The total number of stars composing the cluster is estimated at 100,000. Globular star clusters like Omega Centauri play an important role in astronomy when it comes to determining the age of stars. Because all the stars in a cluster

S

must have originated at the same time, they give an exact picture of the stage of development different stars are at after the passage of a given span of time. In this way the age of Omega Centauri has been established at approximately 8 to 10 billion years (see photo, page 130).

The Sun

The Sun is the most important celestial body, without which there could be no life on Earth. Without the continual flow of solar energy, Earth would be a dead, ice-cold ball of rock with an average temperature of minus 270°C. But the Sun has been radiating immense amounts of energy toward Earth for several billion years in the form of visible light. The energy the Sun emits is enough to make all the water on Earth's surface—all the oceans, icebergs, rivers, and lakes—evaporate within 10 seconds! But because of the huge distance that separates the Sun from Earth, only about one half of one billionth of the Sun's radiation reaches Earth. This still amounts to 1.5 quintillion kilowatt-hours annually.

The Sun is the star that is closest to Earth. Just like all other stars, which are much farther away, it generates energy and produces its own light. Compared to other stars, it is a rather insignificant, small specimen with only average mass, luminosity, and energy production. All the other bright stars that can be seen well with the unaided eye are clearly larger and more luminous—in many cases dramatically so (see Antares, page 69, Arcturus, page 36, and Deneb, pages 44–45).

Still, in comparison to Earth, the Sun's dimensions are overwhelmingly large. It is assumed

that the Sun derives its energy from a process of thermonuclear fusion that goes on at its core. There temperatures of around 16 million degrees and a pressure of about 200 billion atmospheres prevail. Under these conditions, hydrogen atoms (which make up most of the Sun's matter) fuse into helium, a process during which minute quantities of mass are converted into energy in accordance with Albert Einstein's famous equation: energy equals mass times the speed of light squared, or $E = mc^2$. The Sun thus "uses up" about 4 million tons of mass per second, but it is so staggeringly large that from the time of its infancy it has converted only about .03 percent of its mass into energy.

The Sun is the only star on whose surface we are able to detect specific features. The most famous of these is the sunspots, relatively cool regions in the Sun's surface that appear dark because the temperature there is lower. In these sunspots huge eruptions often take place, during which radiation and matter are flung out into space. These eruptions are responsible for the famous northern and southern lights on Earth. They also can lead to radio blackouts, and they affect the upper atmosphere in various ways, many of which are not yet completely understood.

The number of sunspots— and consequently the Sun's activity—varies. Sunspots come in cycles of about 11 years. The causes of these sunspot cycles and of many other processes taking place on the Sun's surface are still mysterious. At present, the Sun is approaching a relatively inactive phase. The last period of maximum sunspots was at the end of 1989; the next

minimum is expected around the year 1994. A new maximum of activity accompanying high numbers of sunspots is due around the year 2000.

Basic Data of the Sun

Diameter:	870,000 miles (1.4 million km) (109 times that of Earth)
Distance from Earth (mean):	93 million miles (149.6 million km)
Mass:	2 septillion (2×10^{27}) tons or 333,000 times Earth's mass
Age:	ca. 5 billion years
Surface temperature:	5,800°C
Total energy output:	380,000 quintillion (10^{18}) kilowatts

Because of its tremendous importance for Earth, the Sun always has been an object of religious veneration. Many old cultures had sun gods, and even today the Sun is often invoked as a symbol of life and strength, as at summer and winter solstice celebrations in mid-June and mid-December, respectively. (For more on these dates and the seasons in general, see pages 13 and 104.)

Supernovas

Among the most spectacular but unfortunately also the rarest phenomena to be observed in the sky are the supernovas. A star suddenly blazes up, becomes incredibly bright and outshines all other stars for some weeks or months. In the current millenium, only six supernovas visible to the naked eye have occurred, namely in the years 1006 in the constellation Lupus (see pages 96–97), 1054 in Taurus, 1181 and 1572 in Cassiopeia (see pages 28–29), 1604 in Ophiuchus (see pages 66–67), and 1987 in the Large Magellanic Cloud (see page 137). Through telescopes, about another 400 supernovas have been seen in distant galaxies (see page 135).

Supernovas seem to come out of nowhere and were therefore dubbed "new stars" (from Latin *nova*, see page 142), but in effect these stars existed all along in a much more inconspicuous and much less bright form before blazing up so dramatically. Within a few weeks, such a star suddenly generates the equivalent of energy it would take our Sun billions of years to manufacture; its outer parts literally are torn apart and pour into space at tremendous speeds. Astronomers therefore think that the appearance of a supernova marks the death of an especially heavy star. When a star has exhausted all means of generating energy, it eventually collapses. In this sudden and chaotic collapse of the star's core, unimaginable quantities of energy are released. The innermost parts remain as a neutron star, whereas the outer ones survive as gas nebulas, thus enriching the interstellar material from which new stars may form later. But not all stars end life this way. Smaller ones like our Sun lose their light in a much less spectacular fashion.

There are still many unsolved questions concerning the phenomenon of supernovas. To some of these questions, astronomers hope, the analysis of detailed observations made during the supernova in the Large Magellanic Cloud in 1987 will yield answers. There is one aspect of all this that is particularly in-triguing. The immense amount of energy involved in a supernova eruption releases various elements from the core of the dying star, elements that were formed there millions of years ago. In the course of the explosion new elements are formed as well, such as carbon, oxygen, and nitrogen, and metals, such as iron, nickel, and cobalt. All elements except for hydrogen, which still makes up 90 percent of all the matter in space today, were hurled into space a very long time ago by supernova explosions, and they are what is the foundation of life. We thus owe our existence to the supernovas of past astronomical ages.

Variable Stars

Many stars do not always exhibit the same brightness. Instead they change their magnitude in cycles anywhere from several hours to several years in length, but most commonly with a so-called period of up to 100 days. In many of these variable stars the magnitudinal fluctuations occur with considerable regularity, whereas in others they follow no clearly recognizable pattern.

There are two reasons for the fluctuations in brightness. Either the physical characteristics of the star change—it may be growing larger or smaller or its surface temperature may rise and drop—or the star is concealed by another star that stands in our direct line of vision—as the Sun is hidden by the Moon in a solar eclipse—and blocks the light of the star behind it from our view for a certain period. The stars that change in brightness for the first reason are called intrinsic variables, and the most famous one of them is Mira in the constellation Cetus (see pages 74 and 140). The second group consists of stars called eclipsing binaries. Their most famous representative is Algol, the Demon Star in the constellation Perseus (see pages 30–31). Eclipsing binaries also could be considered as a subgroup of the spectroscopic binaries (see page 132) whose component stars cannot be seen separately through a telescope. However, their existence is revealed not only by characteristic changes in their color spectrum but also by the orientation of their orbits, on which they can mutually obscure each other for the viewer on Earth. Only few variable stars can be detected by the naked-eye stargazer, which is why, apart from Mira and Algol, only the following are marked in the star maps:

• **Delta Cephei** Although this star was known to the astronomers of antiquity because of its brightness, the changes in magnitude were not noticed until 1784, when the Englishman Goodricke discovered the star's variability. This is all the more surprising because the fluctuation can be detected with the unaided eye, as can that of Algol. Delta Cephei is a huge star, one of the so-called supergiants. It shines 3,300 times more brightly than the Sun. The fluctuation occurs in an extremely regular cycle of 5 days, 8 hours, and 48 minutes as Delta Cephei alternately expands and contracts, with a resulting change in diameter of 6 percent. The surface temperature and the radiating surface area fluctuate as well, and consequently, of course, the star's brightness. Delta Cephei is an intrinsic variable. It is about 1,200 light-years away from Earth.

• **L 2 Puppis** is also an intrinsic variable. It resembles Mira (see

V

pages 140–41). Its brightness fluctuates within a period of 141 days. At a distance of 200 light-years it shines with a mean intrinsic luminosity that is 200 times greater than the Sun's.

• **Epsilon Aurigae** is an eclipsing binary and one of the most mysterious star systems. Its period of fluctuation is the longest of all known eclipsing binary stars, 9,885 days. This means it takes approximately 27 years for the star to change from maximum brightness to minimum brightness and back to maximum again! The main star of Epsilon Aurigae is relatively well known (1,900 light-years distant; 60,000 times brighter than the Sun), but its companion is still shrouded in mystery. To date, no trace of it has been detected despite the fact that it covers the gigantic main star, which has a diameter 100 times as large as the Sun's, for two years, the period of the variable star's minimum brightness. The unknown companion consequently has to be at least 1,500 times, or perhaps as much as 3,000 times, larger than the Sun. This would make it larger than any star we know. At this point astronomers consider it more likely, however, that this companion is a still young, hot star enveloped in a huge cloud of gas and dust out of which it was born and which is still so opaque that it obscures the light of the main star for over two years. The next obscuring of Epsilon Aurigae is expected to occur in the years 2009 to 2011.

Vega

This, the brightest star in the constellation Lyra and also the most conspicuous star of the Summer Triangle, is one of those stars that has nothing particularly unusual in its physical makeup but that is interesting for historical reasons.

In relation to the Sun, Vega is a distance of 25 light-years away, its diameter is three times as large, and its mass is four times as big. Vega's intrinsic luminosity is 45 times greater than that of the Sun.

Vega was the first star in the history of astronomy to be photographed. The photograph was taken on July 16, 1850 at the Harvard Observatory with an exposure time of 100 seconds and was made possible through the recently invented daguerreotype process. Vega's role as north star lies considerably farther back in the past. About 12,000 years ago the north celestial pole, which describes a very slow, large circle in the sky, was in the vicinity of Vega (see page 42). Polaris fulfills this function considerably better, however, for Vega was nine times farther from the pole than Polaris is.

Venus

The Roman goddess of love lent her name to the Sun's second closest planet. Venus approaches Earth closer than any other heavenly body except for the Moon and consequently shines very brightly in the sky. Its brilliant presence as the morning and the evening star (see pages 115–16) makes it a particularly striking object that always has seemed worthy of special veneration.

Modern astronomy has shown, however, that the conditions on the planet's surface do not resemble the image of the goddess of love in the remotest. Venus has a hellish landscape with surface temperatures of between 400 and 500°C (about 900°F) and an air pressure more than 90 times that on Earth. This kind of environment causes metals like tin and lead to melt, and the first space probes that were lowered through the planet's atmosphere survived these conditions only for a few hours.

The reason for the extreme heat on Venus is the planet's atmosphere. Unlike Earth's atmosphere, it is composed almost entirely—at least 98 percent—of carbon dioxide. Thus Venus represents an extreme example of the same greenhouse effect that is now causing general alarm on Earth. For it is the nature of carbon dioxide to let incoming sunlight pass through but trap heat radiating back in the same way that glass roofs do in greenhouses. It is this mechanism that heats up Venus's surface to such extreme temperatures.

There is of course no life on Venus, given the conditions that exist there. The planet's surface is known at this point only through detailed radar measurements, which show mountain ranges and plains. Venus's surface cannot be examined through a telescope because the planet's atmosphere is not transparent (see photo, page 148). Astronomers are gaining more insight from data sent back by the spacecraft Magellan launched toward Venus on May 4, 1989.

Basic Data of Venus

Distance to the Sun:	67.2 million miles (108.2 million km)
Period of revolution about the Sun:	224 days
Diameter:	7,517 miles (12,104 km)
Period of rotation:	243 days
Mass:	.81 times that of Earth

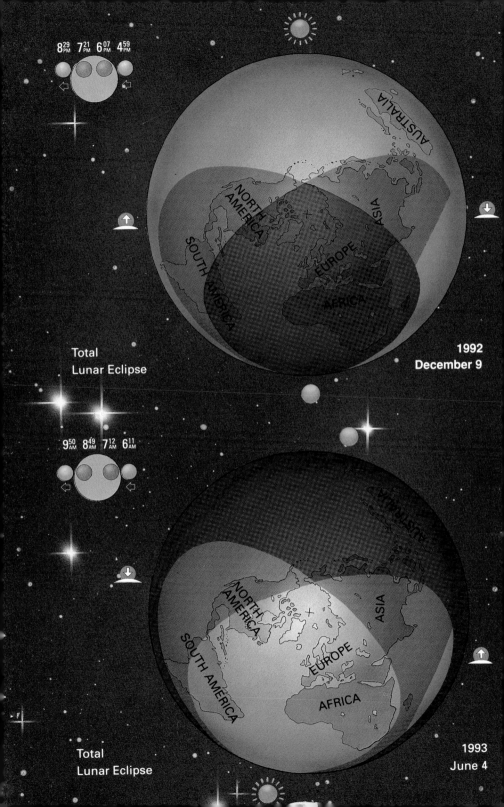

8:29 PM 7:21 PM 6:07 PM 4:59 PM

Total
Lunar Eclipse

1992
December 9

9:50 AM 8:49 AM 7:12 AM 6:11 AM

Total
Lunar Eclipse

1993
June 4

What do the maps of lunar eclipses on the following pages show?

Moon

Night side: Eclipse visible from beginning to end

Moon sets during the eclipse

Moon rises during the eclipse

Shortly before the eclipse ends

Shortly after the eclipse has begun

The Moon rising: Shortly before the eclipse ends

The Moon setting: Shortly after the eclipse has begun

Day side: Eclipse not visible

Sun

The Moon passing through Earth's umbra

Moon

Earth's umbra

How Do I Use the Maps?

The maps on the foldout back flap show all the total lunar eclipses up to the year 2000. In a lunar eclipse, the Moon travels from west to east through Earth's circular umbra. The small drawings at the upper left show the exact times in EST of the eclipse. A lunar eclipse looks the same from all points on Earth where the Moon is above the horizon. The large maps of the globe, with the north pole at the center (the continents appear distorted), indicate where a given lunar eclipse can be seen. Where the Sun is shining at that time and it is day, the eclipse is invisible. On the night side, where it is full moon, one can see the eclipse for the full period. But because Earth rotates, there are two zones between the day side and the night side where the Moon is rising or setting while it is still moving through Earth's umbra. Inhabitants of these areas therefore witness either the end of the eclipse or its beginning. For more on lunar eclipses, see page 112.

159

Planetaria and Observatories

United States

Grace H. Flandrau Planetarium
University of Arizona
Cherry and University
  Boulevard
Tucson, Arizona 85721

Planetarium
Griffith Observatory
2800 E. Observatory Road
Los Angeles, California 90027

Reuben H. Fleet Space Theater
  and Science Center
Balboa Park, P.O. Box 33303
San Diego, California 92103

Alexander Morrison Planetarium
California Academy of
  Sciences
Golden Gate Park
San Francisco, California
  94118

Charles C. Gates Planetarium
Museum of Natural History
2201 Colorado Blvd.,
  City Park
Denver, Colorado 80205

Alexander Brest Planetarium
Museum of Science and
  History
1025 Gulf Life Drive
Jacksonville, Florida 32207

Jim Cherry Memorial
  Planetarium
Fernbank Science Center
156 Heaton Park Drive, N.E.
Atlanta, Georgia 30307

The Adler Planetarium
1300 S. Lake Shore Drive
Chicago, Illinois 60605

Arnim D. Hummel Planetarium
Eastern Kentucky University
Richmond, Kentucky 40475

Davis Planetarium
Maryland Science Center
601 Light Street
Baltimore, Maryland 21230

Charles Hayden Planetarium
Boston Museum of Science
Science Park
Boston, Massachusetts 02114

Abrams Planetarium
Michigan State University
East Lansing, Michigan 48824

McDonnell Star Theater
St. Louis Science Center
5100 Clayton Road,
  Forest Park
St. Louis, Missouri 63110

American Museum Hayden
  Planetarium
Central Park West
  at 81st Street
New York, New York 10024

Morehead Planetarium
University of North Carolina-
  Chapel Hill
Morehead Building CB #3480
Chapel Hill, North Carolina
  27599

Fels Planetarium
Franklin Institute Science
  Museum
20th and The Parkway
Philadelphia, Pennsylvania
  19103

Universe Planetarium/Space
  Theater
Science Museum of Virginia
2500 West Broad Street
Richmond, Virginia 23220

Canada

Margret Zeidler Star Theatre
Edmonton Space Sciences
  Centre
11211 - 142 Street
Edmonton, Alberta
CANADA T5M 4A1

H.R. MacMillan Planetarium
British Columbia Space
  Sciences Society
Vanier Park, 1100 Chestnut
  Street
Vancouver, British Columbia
CANADA V6J 3J9

Dow Planetarium
1000 rue Saint-Jacques Ouest
Montreal, Quebec
CANADA, H3C 1G7

Credits

English translation © Copyright 1992 by
Barron's Educational Series, Inc.

© Copyright 1990 by Gräfe and Unzer Verlag
GmbH, Munich, Germany
The title of the German book is *Sterne und Planeten*

Translated from the German by Rita and Robert Kimber

All inquiries should be addressed to:
Barron's Educational Series, Inc.
250 Wireless Boulevard
Hauppauge, NY 11788

Library of Congress Catalog Card No. 91-42143

International Standard Book No. 0-8120-4776-1

Library of Congress Cataloging-in-Publication Data
Ekrutt, Joachim W.
  [Sterne und Planeten. English]
   Stars and planets : identifying them, learning about them,
experiencing them, with all important celestial events up to the
year 2000 / Joachim Ekrutt ; and with a lexicon of celestial
bodies, 175 star maps, pictures of the constellations, and dia-
grams, 30 color photos of celestial objects, star maps, and
diagrams by Wil Tirion ; maps of solar and lunar eclipses by
Heiner O. Neuendorf ; [translated from the German by Rita and
Robert Kimber].
      p.   cm.
   Translation of: Sterne und Planeten.
   Includes index.
   ISBN 0-8120-4776-1
   1. Astronomy—Observer's manuals. 2. Stars—Observer's
manuals. 3. Planets—Observer's manuals.
I. Title.
QB63.E3813   1992
523—dc20
                                             91-42143
                                                 CIP

PRINTED IN HONG KONG

6 7 8 9 0   9927   13 12 11 10 9

Credits

Photo credits:
Work collective ASTRO-FOTO, Alt, Brodkorb, Rihm, Rusche: Front cover, pages 5, 24, 25 (left), 147, 152, 153; TREUGESELL publisher: book spine, pages 10, 18, 25 (right), 129, 140; NASA/ Bader Planetarium: pages 132, 139, 148; European Southern Observatory (ESO): pages 130, 136; NASA/J.P.L.: Front cover, pages 6, 7, 135, 144; SAO/US Naval Observatory: pages 17, 26, 52, 78; Doring: Front cover, page 109; Dreesen: page 110; Jim McCarthy: page 118.

Scientific Advisor:
Rahlf Hansen, Dipl. Phys.
Position of planets: Hartwig Lüthen

Drawings:
Solar and lunar eclipses on flaps at front and back: Heiner O. Neuendorf; Star maps and diagrams: Wil Tirion

Illustrations of constellations:
from *Johannis Hevelii uranographia totum coelum stellatum,* Danzig, 1690 (reprint: Taschkent, 1978)

The author:
Joachim Ekrutt, Ph.D. has for many years been on the staff of the Hamburg Planetarium. He is also a contributor to the magazines *Stern* and *GEO* and the author of an illustrated reference volume on the Sun and of the Barron's Mini Fact Finder *Stars*.

Index

Little Dipper, 38
Longitude, 14
Lunar eclipses, 112–113
Lunar phases, 105–107
Lupus (the Wolf), 96–97
Lynx, 63
Lyra, **78**

M 7 (star cluster), 148
Magellanic Clouds, 100–103, 135, 137
Magnitude, 134
Mars, 69, 116, 117, 137, 139
Maximum elongation, 114
Mercury, 114–115, 132, 137–138
Messier, Charles, 21, 73, 135, 148
Meteorites, 138
Meteors, 138–139
Meteor showers, 138, 139
Milky Way, 21, 28, 36, 40–41, 48, 69, 90, 92, 94, 135, 137, 140
Mira, 74, 140–141
Mizar, 33, 132
Moon, 11, 16, 50, 68, 109, 141
  lunar eclipses, 112–113
  phases of, 105–107

Nebulas, 21, 141–142
Neptune, 145
North celestial pole, 8
Northern Crown, 36–37
Northern Hemisphere, 10, 13, 22
Northern lights, 142
North Pole, 9
North Star, 22, 34–35, 43
Novas, 47, 142–143

Octans, 88–89
Omega Centauri, 87, 148–149
Ophiuchus, 55, 66–67, 92
Opposition, 114
Orion, 54–55, 69, 100, 131

Pavo, 90, 91
Pavo (the Peacock), 80
Pegasus, 72–73
Penumbra, 108–110, 112
Perseids, 68, 94, 139

Perseus, 30–31, 68, 94
Phoenix, 80, 99
Pisces (the Fish), 74–75
Piscis Austrinus (the Southern Fish), 73, 94–95
Planets, 16–17, 143–145
  appearance in constellations of zodiac, 113–117
  light of, 23–24
Pleiades, 145, 147
Pluto, 145
Polaris, 22, 34–35
Polar night, 13
Pollux, 58
Praesepe, 25, 59, 145
Precession, 43, 70–71
Procyon, 145

Regulus, 60–61
Rigel, 146

Sagitta, 47
Sagittarius (the Archer), 92–93
Saturn, 116, 117, 144, 146
Schiller, Julius, 91, 93
Scorpius, 69, 92
Seasons, 13, 104
Serpens, 66
Sextans, 89
Shooting stars, 138
Sirius, 56, 57, 146–147
Small Magellanic Cloud, 100–101, 135
Solar eclipses, 108–111
Solar system, 17
Solstice, 105
South celestial pole, 8
Southern Cross, 22, 84–85
Southern Hemisphere, 13, 22, 80
Southern lights, 142
Southern Triangle, 90
South Pole, 9
Spica, 38–39
Star clusters, 21, 147
  H and chi Persei, 148
  Hyades, 50, 135
  IC 2602, 83, 87, 148
  M 7, 148
  Omega Centauri, 87, 148–149
  Pleiades, 145, 147
  Praesepe, 25, 59, 145

Star maps, 19–20
  identification tips, 23–24
  series N I, 27–51
  series N II, 53–77
  series S, 79–103
  star designations in, 21
  symbols used in, 21–22
  which stars to look for first, 22–23
Stars:
  binary, 36, 39, 44, 131–133
  circumpolar, 10
  fixed, 10–11, 51, 134–135
  globular clusters, 87
  multiple, 21
  variable, 21, 150–151
Summer Triangle, 44, 46, 68
Sun, 11–12, 149
  ecliptic path of, 15–16, 42, 66, 71
  solar eclipses, 108–111
Supernovas, 67, 85, 97, 103, 149–150

Taurus (the Bull), 48, 50
Thuban, 43
Time zones, 14–15, 19
Triangulum Australe, 90
Triangulum (the Triangle), 103
Tropic of Capricorn, 70, 71
Tucana (the Toucan), 80
Tycho's Star, 31

Umbra, 108–110, 112
Universal Time, 14
Uranometria, 21
Uranus, 144–145
Ursa Major (Great Bear), 23, 32–33, 65, 70
Ursa Minor, 38

Variable stars, 21, 150–151
Vega, 44, 151
Venus, 11, 23, 115–116, 151
Vernal equinox, 105
Vernal Triangle, 34, 36, 60
Virgo, 38
Volans (the Flying Fish), 80

Winter Hexagon, 50, 80

Zenith, 9

Index

Page references in **bold type** indicate color photos.

Achernar, 98, 99, 130
Adhara, 57
Age of Aquarius, 71
Age of Pisces, 71
Albireo, 133
Alcor, 33, 132
Aldebaran, 50–51
Algol, 30, 130, 150
Alpha Centauri, 87, 130–131
Altair, 47
Andromeda Galaxy, **26**, 31, 73, 103, 135, 137
Antares, 69
Aquarius (the Water Bearer), 70–71
Aquila, 46–47
Ara (the Altar), 91
Arcturus, 36, 89, 131
Argo Navis (the Ship of the Argonauts), 82, 88
Aries (the Ram), 76–77
Astronomical calendar 1992–2000, 119–128
Auriga, 48–49
Autumnal equinox, 105
Autumn Square, 72

Bartsch, Jakob, 84
Bayer, Johann, 21, 81, 94, 99, 102, 130
Betelgeuse, 131
Big Dipper, 22, 32–33, 65
Binary stars, 36, 39, 44, 131, 133
  spectroscopic, 132
  visual, 132
Binoculars, 24–25
Boötes, 36, 38
Brahe, Tycho, 31

Cancer (the Crab), 59
Canes Venatici, **25**, 35
Canis Major, 56–57
Canopus, 83, 100, 133
Capella, 48, 133
Capricornus (the Sea Goat), 70, 100
Cassiopeia, 28–29
Castor, 58

Celestial events, 104–117
Centaurus, 84, 86–87, 93, 130
Central European Time, 14
Cetus (the Whale), 29, 30, 74
Chi Persei, 68, 148
Christian Night Sky, The, (Schiller), 91
Circinus, 88
Coalsack Nebula, 84
Colors, 25
Columba, 84
Comets, 133–134
Conjunction, planetary, 114
Constellations:
  history of, 20–21
  origin of, 11
Constellations of the zodiac, 16, 113–117
Cor Caroli, 35
Corvus (the Crow), 65
Cygnus, 44

Daylight saving time, 15
De Lacaille, Nicolas Louis, 88, 90
Delphinus, 47
Delta Cephei, 31, 150
Deneb, 44–45
Denebola, 60, 61
Dorado (the Swordfish), 80
Draco, 42–43
Dusk, phases of, 12

Earth:
  atmosphere of, 11
  rotation on axis, 8, 72
  seasons and axis tilt, 13, 104
Eastern Standard Time, 14, 15
East European Time, 14
Ecliptic path, 15–16, 42, 66, 71
Epsilon Aurigae, 151
Epsilon Eridani, 99
Epsilon Lyrae, 44, 133
Equator, 9
Eques Stellula, 33
Eridanus, 98–99
Eta Carinae:
  nebula, 142
  star, 83, 142

European Southern Observatory, 101

Fixed stars, 10–11, 51, 134–135
Fomalhaut, 94–95
Foucault's pendulum, 8, 15
Fourth magnitude, 19

Galaxies, 21–22, 135
Gemini, 58–59
Gemma, 36–37
Globular clusters, 87
Great Nebula in Orion, **52**, 55, 142
Greenwich Mean Time, 14
Grus (the Crane), 80, 94, 95

Halley, Edmund, 35, 50–51
Halley's Comet, 17, 134, 135
Hamal, 77
Hercules, 40–41, 47, 62
Hevelius, Johannes, 20, 35, 63, 90
Horizon, 9
H Persei, 148
Hyades, 50, 135–136
Hydra (the Water Snake), 62–63, 85, 86, 98
Hydrogen, 134, 143
Hydrus (the Lesser Water Snake), 80, 81

IC 2602 (star cluster), 83, 87, 148

Jupiter, 116, 117, 136

Kepler, Johannes, 67, 84

L2 Puppis, 84, 85, 150–151
Lagoon Nebula, 142
Large Magellanic Cloud, 100–103, 137, **152–153**
Latitude, 14
Leo (the Lion), 49, 60–61
Leonids, 49, 101, 139
Libra (the Scales), 64–65
Light-year, 11

◁ *The Large Magellanic Cloud, the most gorgeous celestial object in the southern sky.*

THE
POWHATAN
INDIANS

THE POWHATAN INDIANS

Melissa McDaniel

CHELSEA JUNIORS

a division of CHELSEA HOUSE PUBLISHERS

FRONTISPIECE: A watercolor of a *werowance* painted by
John White in 1585.

CHAPTER TITLE ORNAMENT: A drawing of the Powhatan god
Okewas.

English-language words that are italicized in the text can
be found in the glossary at the back of the book.

Chelsea House Publishers
EDITORIAL DIRECTOR Richard Rennert
EXECUTIVE MANAGING EDITOR Karyn Gullen Browne
COPY CHIEF Robin James
PICTURE EDITOR Adrian G. Allen
CREATIVE DIRECTOR Robert Mitchell
ART DIRECTOR Joan Ferrigno
PRODUCTION MANAGER Sallye Scott

The Junior Library of American Indians
SENIOR EDITOR Martin Schwabacher

Staff for THE POWHATAN INDIANS
EDITORIAL ASSISTANT Erin McKenna
ASSISTANT DESIGNER Lydia Rivera
PICTURE RESEARCHER Sandy Jones
COVER ILLUSTRATOR Hal Just

First Printing

1 3 5 7 9 8 6 4 2

Library of Congress Cataloging-in-Publication Data

McDaniel, Melissa.
The Powhatan Indians / Melissa McDaniel.
  p. cm.— (The Junior Library of American Indians)
Includes index.
        0-7910-2494-6
        0-7910-2495-4 (pbk.)
1. Powhatan Indians—History—Juvenile Literature. 2. Powhatan Indians—Social Life and Customs—Juvenile Literature. I. Title. II. Series.
E99.P85M33 1995   95-2497
975'.004973—dc20   CIP
                                                           AC

CONTENTS

CHAPTER 1
Two Legends 7

CHAPTER 2
Life in the Tidewater 13

CHAPTER 3
Powhatan Society 23

CHAPTER 4
Powhatan's Empire 35

CHAPTER 5
The Vanishing Tribes 45

PICTURE ESSAY
Pamunkey Pottery Old and New 49

CHAPTER 6
Struggle for Survival 67

Glossary 76

Chronology 77

Index 78

A map showing
the locations of
the Tidewater tribes
of Virginia.

Chapter **1**

Two Legends

In the beginning of time, the Hare created human beings. At first, he kept his new creations in a giant bag in his house. One day, the winds from the four directions visited the Hare's home. They discovered the men and women the Hare had made and wanted to eat them. The Hare scolded the wind for making such a suggestion and sent them away.

The Hare then created water, land, and one great deer to feed upon the land. Still angry at the Hare, the four winds returned, killed the deer, ate it, and left again. The Hare took the hairs from the dead deer's body and spread them out over the earth. Speaking

7

powerful words, he changed each hair into a deer. He then opened his bag of humans and put one man and one woman in each country, creating the beginning of mankind.

This is how a Potomac Indian who lived 400 years ago described the creation of the world. The Potomacs were one of about 30 Indian groups who lived along the Atlantic Ocean near Chesapeake Bay in the present-day states of Virginia and Maryland. These tribes had very similar languages and cultures. Near the end of the 16th century, many of them fell under the rule of Powhatan, the leader of one group. Because Powhatan created an empire that included most of the Indian villages in the area, together they are called the Powhatan tribes.

Although he lent his name to a kingdom containing thousands of people, Powhatan is not the most famous member of the Powhatan tribes. That honor belongs to his daughter Pocahontas, the prime figure in one of the most celebrated stories in American history. The story goes back to the very beginning of the English *colonial* efforts in America.

In 1607, British colonists founded Jamestown, the first permanent English settlement in North America. Jamestown was located on the James River in what is now Virginia, right in the heart of Powhatan's

An oil painting of Pocahontas dressed as an English noblewoman. Pocahontas, the daughter of Powhatan, married an Englishman and met the queen of England.

territory. While exploring the surrounding area, one of the settlement's leaders, Captain John Smith, was captured by Native Americans. According to Smith, he was taken to Powhatan's village and forced to kneel on a stone altar. Just when an Indian warrior was about to smash his skull with a heavy club, Pocahontas, who was then about 12 years old, flung herself over his body, protecting him from harm. She pleaded with her father to spare Smith's life. Powhatan, who adored his young daughter, relented, allowing Smith to leave unscathed.

As legend has it, Pocahontas also helped the starving colonists by convincing her fellow tribespeople to provide them with food. This food enabled the Jamestown colony to survive the harsh early months of 1608. Because of her generosity, Pocahontas is said to have rescued not only Smith but the entire colony. And because Jamestown survived, she made possible the development of the United States of America.

For centuries, the story of Pocahontas's rescue of John Smith was believed to be true. But now many historians think it is inaccurate. Some believe that Smith was actually experiencing a ritualized adoption ceremony making him a member of Powhatan's tribe. Others believe that the event never happened at all because Smith did not mention Pocahontas in print until 1624, the third time he wrote about his captivity by the Indians. In Smith's earlier accounts, he wrote that Powhatan had treated him kindly and released him.

Though the legend of Pocahontas is well known, the story of her father, her people, and their relations with the first British settlers in North America has been told much less often. Yet the history of the Tidewater Indians, both before and after the arrival of the Europeans, is as full of drama and conflict as the legends surrounding Pocahontas.

Four centuries after their first contact with the English colonists, members of these proud tribes are still living in the state of Virginia. There they continue to keep alive the complex and fascinating society they created long before white people ever set foot in America. ▲

*An engraving by Theodore
de Bry, published in 1590,
shows Tidewater Indians
making a canoe by
burning and scraping
out the inside of a log.*

Chapter 2

Life in the Tidewater

The Powhatan tribes lived in the part of Virginia known as the Tidewater. This region earned its name because the many rivers flowing through the coastal lowlands into Chesapeake Bay are affected by the tides. Their water is a mixture of fresh water and salt water from the ocean.

When the English first arrived, there were at least 14,000 Powhatans living in many small villages in the area. These towns were usually built on high ground along rivers so that the Indians could see others approaching. Where the river water was salty, the Indians made sure their towns were near freshwater springs so they could obtain drinking water. Powhatan towns rarely contained more than 20 houses, which were scattered in groups separated by fields, rather than lined up in rows along streets.

Powhatan houses were shaped like tunnels. They were built by sticking two rows of *saplings* into the ground, bending them over, and tying them together at the top. Poles were tied across the bent saplings to form

A modern replica of a Powhatan home in Jamestown Festival Park, Virginia.

a framework. To make walls and a roof, the framework was covered with mats woven from marsh reeds or bark. Each house consisted of one large room with an entrance at each end. A fire was kept burning in the middle of the house at all times. The smoke escaped through a hole in the roof. If the house was too dark or smoky, some of the mats were rolled up like window blinds, allowing fresh air to flow freely through the house.

Building and maintaining houses was the responsibility of women. They also wove mats and baskets, *tanned* animal hides to make clothing and bags, and made pots, utensils, and tools. Their chief task, however, was farming.

Each spring, Powhatan women, with the help of children and some elderly men, planted corn, beans, squash, and passionflowers in the nearby fields. They put a few kernels of corn and some beans together in mounds of dirt. Other vegetables were planted in between the mounds. One plant, however, was grown apart from the others—tobacco. Tobacco was important in Powhatan religious and political rituals, but it was completely unknown to Europeans before they arrived in the Americas.

The Powhatans planted four types of corn, which ripened at different times. That way, fresh corn was available from early June until October. They would either roast the corn in a fire or grind it up, wrap it in cornhusks, and boil it. They also sucked out the juice from the cornstalks, which was delightfully sweet. Some of the corn was saved to be used as seed the following year. The Powhatans also dried some corn to use during winter by laying it on thick mats in the sun. After it was dried, corn could be boiled for eating or pounded into cornmeal. Cornmeal was used to thicken stews and to make bread. In the summer, women gathered wild strawberries, raspberries, apples, and grapes in the forests. They also dug up wild potatoes. In the fall, they collected walnuts, hickory nuts, chestnuts, and acorns. These nuts were eaten raw or dried for future use. They could also be boiled to make delicacies like "walnut milk," a pudding made from ground-up hickory nuts and water. On special occasions, squash was added to walnut milk. The nuts collected by the women also provided the tribes with valuable oils that were used in cooking and as medicines.

While the women were tending the fields and gathering, and drying food, the men

An engraving by Theodore de Bry showing Powhatan Indians drying fish to store for the winter.

were hunting and fishing. Canoes were vital to the Powhatans' success as fishermen. Each canoe was made from a single log. The log was hollowed out by using stone axes or by burning sections and then scraping away the soft, charred wood. Some of these canoes were 50 feet long and could hold 40 people, along with their paddles, fishing gear, and temporary shelters.

The Powhatans used many methods to catch fish, both from land and from canoes. Sometimes they used rods with hooks made of bone. They also used nets made from deer *sinew*, tree bark, or rope that the women had spun by hand from plant fibers. Fishermen shot fish with arrows tied to cords and speared fish that were in shallow water. They also made traps called weirs by placing stones across the river in the shape of a V. When the fish swam into the point of the V, they were caught in a large wicker trap.

Fish were either roasted on a frame over a fire or boiled in a stew. They could be smoked and dried by moving the cooking frame farther from the fire. Smoked fish often lasted more than a month before going bad.

Although fishing provided the Powhatans with a regular source of food, men took more pride in hunting, which supplied not only food but also skins for clothing. Hunting required great skill in the dense, dark woods of the Tidewater. Men often hunted alone, using a wooden bow with a string made of twisted deerskin or animal gut. Their arrows had points made of bird beaks, bones, antlers, or stones. Sometimes hunters disguised themselves as deer in order to get closer to their prey. After stuffing the head of a deerskin, a hunter would drape the rest of the skin over his arm. If a deer looked up when a hunter approached, the hunter would move the dead deer's head to mimic a live deer. Seeing another deer, the prey remained calm, rather than fleeing as it would at the sight of a human. This enabled the hunter to take careful aim.

Another hunting method required many men working together. When hunters encountered a herd of deer, they would form a large circle around it. Then they built fires and began shouting. The deer would dart between the fires, trying to run away, only to find the hunters there ready to shoot them. By surrounding a herd, a group of hunters could kill up to 15 deer at a time. If a herd was on a point of land jutting into the water, a similar method was used. Some of the men cut off the deer's escape route, forcing the deer into the water, where hunters in canoes were waiting for them.

The Powhatans also hunted muskrats, rabbits, squirrels, raccoons, opossums, and wild turkeys, and they trapped beavers and otters. Bear was valued both as a gourmet delicacy and for the oil from its fat, which was used to make paint for their bodies.

Hunting provided the skins that the Powhatans used for clothing. But because of the warm climate, they often wore very little. Young girls wore no clothes at all until they reached *puberty.* Both men and women usually wore nothing but *loincloths* made from deerskin or grass. For hunting or war expeditions, deerskin leggings and moccasins were added to the costume. Wealthier people wore leather robes embroidered with shells and beads.

Even in winter, the Powhatans went as long as possible without wearing extra layers of clothing. They preferred to simply adjust to the cold. Children were prepared for this right from the start. After a baby was born, it was dipped in water, regardless of how cold the season. Throughout their early years, children were washed every day, and their skin was oiled and painted to make it better able to withstand the cold. Sometimes adults also oiled their bodies to help keep themselves warm. When they could endure the cold no longer, they donned fur cloaks. In winter, the rich wore warm, shiny robes made from woven feathers.

Throughout the summer months when food was plentiful, the Powhatans spent most evenings making music, dancing, and playing games. The Powhatans played deerskin drums, flutes fashioned from cane, and rattles made from dried gourds. They also wrestled, held footraces, and had contests to see who could kick a ball the farthest. Men played a game similar to field hockey, in which they used sticks to hit a leather ball between two trees that served as the goal. Women and boys played a game similar to soccer.

As the weather grew colder, the tribes prepared for their annual winter hunt. They stored dried food on mat-covered *scaffolds* next to their houses or in holes they dug in the woods. Everyone except the very old and the very young moved west, where there were more deer. Women carried the household items and rolled-up mats to make new houses, leaving the men free to be on constant alert for game or enemies. Men spent the winter days hunting, while women set up temporary camps, cooked, and tanned skins.

In early spring, the Powhatans gathered their belongings and returned to their permanent villages, and the cycle of planting and hunting began again. By adapting and adjusting to the changing seasons, they enjoyed a varied way of life that satisfied all their physical needs. ▲

An engraving of the god Okewas, whom the Powhatans considered so powerful that they carried images of him into battle.

Chapter 3

Powhatan Society

The Powhatan tribes had a complex society consisting of many different ranks. There were priests, councillors, and ruling families who were much wealthier than ordinary people.

Each tribe was ruled by a leader called a *werowance* or, if a woman, a *weronsqua*. These positions were passed down through families. But rather than passing the title from father to son, the Powhatans used a type of matrilineal succession, meaning the title was passed through women. The order of succession went from the werowance's mother's oldest son to the youngest, then from her oldest daughter to the youngest. When there were no more living children, the title passed to her oldest daughter's firstborn son. Thus women could be leaders, but only if they had no surviving brothers.

Werowances had great wealth, most of it obtained through *tribute* paid by the common people. Tribute given to werowances included skins, corn, game, and copper. This wealth enabled them to have sumptuous lifestyles. They ate lavish meals and wore warm, elaborately decorated robes. Their houses were much larger than those of ordinary people; some were 40 yards long. A werowance's house had an entrance only at one end. A visitor had to walk through long, dark passageways before coming to the chamber where the ruler greeted guests.

Accompanying this great wealth was near absolute power, including life-and-death power over their subjects. Minor offenses could bring swift beatings with a club, while more serious offenses, such as murder, theft from a fellow tribesmember, or disobeying the werowance, were punishable by death. In one case in 1676, a werowance was negotiating with the English. While he was speaking, one of his subjects interrupted him. The werowance raised his tomahawk and split the rude man's head open. He then continued the conversation as if nothing had happened. Most of the time, however, punishments were carried out by an assistant.

The next most prominent members of Powhatan society were *quiyoughcosucks*, or priests. Because it was believed that priests could foretell the future, including whether raids would be successful, they were valued advisers to the werowances. Priests were thought to be able to control the weather and confuse enemies during warfare. They also served as the tribal doctors, using medicinal plants and roots to cure the sick.

Perhaps their most important function was their ability to summon and converse with Okewas, the most powerful god in the Powhatan religion. Okewas was a harsh and *vengeful* spirit whose language only the priests could understand. Sometimes he would appear in the woods in the form of a handsome young man. The Powhatans believed that any trouble they faced, such as illnesses or bad harvests, was a punishment from Okewas. To appease him, they gave him offerings of tobacco, shells, and copper. Okewas was considered so powerful that warriors carried his image into battle.

Images of Okewas were also housed in village temples. Temples were about 100 feet long and aligned in an east-west direction, with a door only on the east end. The first of the many rooms contained a fire that the priests kept lit continuously. The most westerly room contained the bodies of dead werowances and wooden images of Oke-was and other gods. These temples also served as storehouses for the rulers' wealth. Skins, corn, and jewelry were all kept here, guarded by the gods.

Besides the tribal werowances, each village had its own werowance who paid tribute to those above him and received tribute from those beneath him. Below village werowances in rank were councillors, men who gained prestige and wealth through their exploits in hunting or warfare and who advised rulers. Along with priests and werowances, these men comprised the council that declared war.

The Powhatans waged war for revenge, to gain territory, and to *abduct* women and children. Although men who were captured during warfare were usually tortured and killed, women, children, and rulers were often adopted into the tribe.

The Powhatans wore elaborate jewelry and other decorations, which often indicated a person's status in society. Beads made from shells were commonly used to make earrings, necklaces, headbands, and embroidery for clothing. Copper was more rare and was worn solely by the rich. Only certain

A 1586 watercolor by John White of a tribal priest, or quiyoughcosuck. The small lock of hair behind his ear showed his rank.

chiefs were allowed to wear headbands made of copper.

Both men and women usually had their ears pierced two or three times, but the fancier and more flamboyant earrings were reserved for men. In addition to beads, men wore earrings made of birds' feet and bear and cougar claws, which were sometimes decorated with copper. John Smith reported seeing a man wearing as an earring "a small greene and yellow coloured snake, neare halfe a yard in length, which crawling and lapping her selfe about his necke oftentimes familiarly would kisse his lips. Others weare a dead Rat tyed by the taile."

While men had the more elaborate earrings, only women wore tattoos. To make tattoos, they slit their skin with a heated knife and rubbed soot into the cut. Women covered their faces and bodies with tattoos of plants, flowers, and animals.

Both men and women regularly painted their faces and shoulders with dyes derived from plants, minerals, and oils. Some colors and designs were reserved for special occasions. Although red was the most common color of paint, especially for women, men sometimes wore yellow, black, or white.

Like jewelry, a person's hairstyle indicated his or her place in society. Until puberty, girls wore their hair very short in the front and on the sides but very long in the back. In some parts of Powhatan territory, married women wore their hair all one length, cut just below the ears. In other areas, however, they had short bangs and one long braid in back.

Men shaved the hair on the right side of their heads to keep it from getting tangled with their bowstrings. On the left side, they let their hair grow very long—sometimes up to four feet. After combing and greasing their hair with walnut oil to make it sleek, they usually tied it into a knot. The knot was decorated with feathers, or sometimes with deer antlers, shells, or copper *crescents*. The hairstyle of priests was even more unusual. They shaved the right side of their head but allowed one tuft of hair to grow near their right ear.

Parents began training their children at a very young age for their roles in this complicated society. Both mothers and fathers taught boys to hunt. Each morning, a boy's mother would throw moss in the air for him to shoot arrows at, refusing him breakfast until he hit it.

Some time between the ages of 10 and 15, the most promising boys—those who would become priests and councillors—went through an initiation into manhood known as the *Huskenaw*. To begin the ceremony, everyone in the village joined in a morning-long dance and feast in the woods. Dressed in their finest clothes, the Indians danced in circles around a fire. A group of men wearing black horns on their heads and holding green branches stood in the middle. Occasionally during the dance, these men would emit horrible noises, hurl their branches away, and descend upon a small tree and tear it down. They then resumed dancing in the center of the circle.

When everyone was thoroughly exhausted, the boys to be initiated, who were painted white, were brought into the circle. They were ceremonially captured amid much weeping and moaning from the women in the audience. After a great feast, the boys were symbolically killed, and older men danced around their bodies as they lay on the ground. The initiates were then taken into the woods for nine months. They were given a drug, perhaps jimsonweed, which seemed to inspire madness and was supposed to make them forget their previous lives. Having been ritually killed, they were reborn as men and returned to their village. Because they were supposed to remember nothing of their families, it was thought that their loyalty would be only to Okewas and their werowance.

When girls reached puberty, they were considered ready for marriage. Courtship involved a man giving a woman game he had killed, which was supposed to persuade her that he was a good provider. When a woman accepted a marriage proposal, her suitor visited her parents to negotiate a bride-price—the valuable goods he would give her family. After gathering the items he would need to set up a household—a house, pots, bedding—he delivered the bride-price to his fiancée's parents and returned home. The bride then traveled to the groom's new house, where her father joined the couple's hands. The groom's father broke a string of beads over the couple's heads. They were now married.

Marriage brought a man status because it meant that he was mature and capable of providing for others. A man could have more than one wife, but he was expected to be able to support all of them. Thus marriage to more than one woman brought greater status because it indicated greater wealth and hunting ability. Sometimes second and third marriages were meant to be temporary. The couple agreed to stay together for only a year; if they remained together longer, the marriage was expected to be permanent. Both husbands and wives could have affairs, and divorce was also permitted.

Like most aspects of Powhatan culture, the way people were buried depended on their status in society. Ordinary people were wrapped in mats and skins and buried with a

The bodies of dead werowances were preserved and kept in the Powhatans' temples. A model of Okewas watched over the corpses.

few of their possessions. The deceased's female relatives painted their faces black and wailed loudly for a day. In some cases, corpses were placed on a high platform. Every few years, the bones would be taken down and buried together in a large pit.

When a werowance died, his bones were removed from his body, cleaned, and then put back into his skin, which was preserved. The body was put in the village temple alongside the bodies of past werowances. It was believed that only werowances and priests went to the afterlife, a lovely place with plentiful fruits and berries.

In this highly *stratified* society, one man—Powhatan—stood above all others. He was not just a werowance but a *mamanatowick*, or "great king." He had inherited power over eight tribes, and by the end of the 16th century, he had brought another 20 tribes under his control. The werowances of all these tribes paid him tribute. He had many houses and huge fields that were tended by his subjects just for his use. He also had more wives than anyone else—by some accounts more than 100. He kept about a dozen wives at one time. Most of them only stayed with him until bearing a child. After that, they would either return to their villages or be given to a faithful councillor.

When the English colonists arrived in 1607, Powhatan had already gained control over most of the region and was reaching the peak of his power. If the newcomers were going to survive in the Tidewater, they would have to deal with him. ▲

A 19th-century painting showing the arrival of the Jamestown colonists in Powhatan's realm.

Chapter **4**

Powhatan's Empire

The first contact between Europeans and Native Americans in the Chesapeake Bay region most likely took place in the 1520s, when Spanish and Portuguese ships arrived in the area. These travelers were just explorers, however, who did not try to build settlements.

But around 1560, the Spanish decided to establish a colony in the area. They kidnapped a young Indian and taught him Spanish so he could serve as an interpreter. They also baptized the young man as a Christian and renamed him Don Luis. In 1570, Don Luis returned to the Tidewater accompanied by a group of *missionaries,* people who want to convert others to their religion. Don Luis soon left the missionaries because he wanted to live among his own people. The Spanish priests pressured him to return to their *mission.* This angered him, and in 1571 he led a war party to the mission, killing all the Spanish except one young boy. Seeking to avenge the death of the priests, the Spanish attacked the next year, killing 30 Indians. This ended the first disastrous interaction between Europeans and Powhatans.

In the 1580s, the English began trying to colonize the area. Their first attempts failed, but in the spring of 1607, three British ships sailed into Chesapeake Bay and up the James River. They stopped at various villages where the Indians greeted them with great hospitality, often serving them lavish feasts. As a display of friendship, the English gave the Indians gifts of glass beads, bells, and needles. At Appamatuck, the newcomers were met by a man holding a bow and arrow in one hand and a tobacco pipe in the other. He was offering them the choice between war and peace. Although the English did not understand his meaning, they nonetheless correctly chose the pipe. The colonists eventually selected a spot for their new settlement, christening the site Jamestown.

Despite the warm welcome afforded them, the English found the Native Americans perplexing. Unable to distinguish between the various Powhatan groups, the settlers were surprised when some proved friendly while others raided the English fort.

Although suspicious of the English, the Powhatans at first did not consider them a threat because the newcomers hardly even seemed capable of taking care of themselves. The site they had chosen for their settlement lacked drinking water and was near a swamp that would soon be swarming with mosquitoes. By summer, many colonists became ill from drinking bad water. They were also running short of food. Many of the settlers came from the upper classes and felt they were above performing manual labor. Others were businessmen who had traveled to the New World in search of quick money. As a result, the colonists were unwilling or unable to plant the necessary crops. For the Powhatans, providing for oneself and one's family was the highest priority. To them, the English seemed utterly inept.

For a few months, Powhatan simply observed the newcomers. He let each of his tribes deal with the settlers as they saw fit. Had he known that the English were not just visiting but intended to stay, he probably would have destroyed the young colony. But they seemed harmless, and he liked the idea of trading for their metal goods. He also thought they might be useful allies against enemy tribes.

On June 15, 1607, Powhatan finally contacted the Jamestown settlement. He announced to the English that he wanted peace and informed them that he had ordered his tribes to cease raiding the colony. Throughout the summer, Powhatan sent gifts of food to the English.

The condition of the colony worsened, however. About half of the 100 settlers died during the summer. The expected supply ships failed to arrive from England. By fall, the Indians' corn was ripe, and they sold some of it to the starving colonists. But the crops were not plentiful that year. The neighboring

Metal bells and a trade token, which the Jamestown colonists traded to the Powhatans for food and furs.

Indians did not have sufficient supplies to provide the settlers with corn all winter.

John Smith, a member of the colony's governing council, decided to go on trading expeditions to secure corn from tribes that were farther away. He convinced many Indian villages to sell him small portions of their stores. But these Indians also had limited supplies and became less friendly as he kept pestering them for more.

During a December expedition, Smith stumbled across a hunting party led by

This engraving shows Captain John Smith being captured by the Powhatans (top) and a later battle with the Pamunkeys (bottom). Smith's capture in 1607 led to his alleged rescue by Pocahontas.

How they tooke him prisoner in the Oaze 1607.

C. Smith bindeth a faluage to his arm fighteth with the King of Pamaunkee and all his company, and flew 3 of them.

Powhatan's brother Opechancanough and was taken prisoner. Opechancanough took Smith to Werowocomoco, Powhatan's capital city, where Powhatan greeted Smith with great ceremony. During their discussions, Smith told Powhatan of the lands that lay beyond the ocean. When Powhatan asked why the English had come to his territory, Smith lied, saying the English ships had been damaged and forced ashore.

Powhatan told Smith that if the colonists moved from their present settlement to a village closer to him, he would give them food in exchange for metal tools and copper ornaments. He then sent Smith on his way. It was during these conversations, Smith later claimed, that Pocahontas saved him from execution. Although the English did not move their settlement, Powhatan nonetheless kept them well fed, saving the colony from starvation.

But relations between the Powhatans and the English grew worse in the next few years, as the English showed no sign of going home. Each group occasionally conducted raids against the other. Harvests were also bad in these years, causing hardship for both the Indians and the English. Because of their mutual hostility, the Indians were not inclined to sell the colonists corn; they had barely enough to feed themselves. The English, who were better armed, sometimes threatened the Indians, forcing them to surrender their winter food supplies. Powhatan, in turn, tried to take advantage of the settlers' food shortage by demanding guns and swords in exchange for food. Though he was eager to make such trades, he was also more than willing to starve the English out.

By May 1610, the colonists were so desperate that they decided to abandon Jamestown. Powhatan would again have complete control over his empire. But the day after the English set sail for home, they encountered a ship from a fleet bringing supplies and 300 new settlers. With these reinforcements, they turned around and went back to Jamestown.

The new settlers were more hostile toward the Powhatans. They destroyed the Indians' fields and temples and burned entire villages. They demolished the town of Paspahegh, killing every Indian they found, including women and children. This broke the most basic rule of Powhatan warfare. The Powhatans fought back as best they could. Although the English may not have realized it, the Indians now considered themselves at war.

In the next few years, the English conquered more Powhatan villages, setting up new settlements and plantations. Because the English now had other trading partners and were growing more food, they were no longer dependent on the Powhatans' corn. The Indians engaged in small raids against English settlements, but these did little to stop the European expansion.

The situation grew worse, and skirmishes continued until April 1613, when a colonist named Samuel Argall kidnapped Pocahontas. She was taken to Jamestown where she was held hostage for about a year. During that time, she was trained in the ways of English culture and became a Christian, taking the name Rebecca. She also fell in love with one of her tutors, a man named John Rolfe.

The couple married in April 1614. Although Powhatan did not attend the wedding, the union brought peace between his people and the colonists. The couple eventually had one son, Thomas. The family went to England in 1616, where Pocahontas was shown off in British society and met the queen. While preparing to return to Virginia the following year, Pocahontas fell ill. She died before she left England.

Meanwhile, too tired to fight, Powhatan left much of the responsibility of ruling to his brothers. He died in April 1618, past the age of 70, ending a reign that had built an empire.

⌃

On March 22, 1622,
the Powhatans rose up
against the Jamestown
colonists, killing 330
settlers in a surprise attack.

Chapter 5

The Vanishing Tribes

With Powhatan's death, the title of mama-natowick passed to his brother Opichapam. However, Opichapam lacked the vigor and *charisma* to lead an empire. The real ruler was Powhatan's brother Opechancanough, who had grown powerful in the last few years of Powhatan's reign.

But even the more forceful Opechan-canough was not able to resist the settlers' expansion when he first assumed power. The last two years of Powhatan's reign had yielded poor harvests, and hunger was widespread. *Epidemics* of smallpox, measles, and influenza also swept through the area. Although these diseases affected both the colonists and the Native Americans, many more Indians than Europeans died from them. Because the diseases had long existed in Europe, the colonists had natural *immunity* to them. But the Powhatans had never been exposed to these diseases before, so their bodies had no resistance to them.

The British presence in the colony was also growing. John Rolfe, Pocahontas's husband, had introduced Brazilian tobacco into Virginia, and it soon became a valuable cash

A drawing of the tobacco plant native to North America (left) and one that Pocahontas's husband John Rolfe imported from Brazil (right). Tobacco farming was a great source of wealth for the English and was largely responsible for the colony's success.

crop. To encourage new settlers, anyone who could pay their way to the New World was given land on which they could grow tobacco. That the land did not belong to the colony did not seem to bother the English. Colonists in search of quick money began arriving in droves. Between 1618 and 1622, the English population in Virginia jumped from 400 to 1,240.

The English also increased their efforts to convert the Powhatans to Christianity. Indian parents were encouraged to send their children to be brought up by British families. In English culture, it was common for children to be sent to boarding schools and thus raised by other people. But this was unheard of among the Powhatans. To them, the idea that someone else was better able to raise their children was insulting. Besides, the Powhatans knew that their children would most likely just be used as a cheap source of labor.

Opechancanough maintained a peaceful and friendly attitude in the face of the colony's expansion and missionary efforts. When an Englishman killed one of his advisers, he did not complain. He had a plan that had been in the works for much too long to ruin casually. Instead, he reaffirmed the truce between the Powhatans and the English. Peace allowed unarmed

Indians to freely enter British settlements to trade and work.

On the morning of Good Friday, March 22, 1622, a large group of Powhatans arrived at various English settlements as they normally would, behaving in a friendly manner. However, at a time set by Opechancanough, the Indians without warning grabbed weapons from the English and attacked them. The English were caught completely off guard. By the day's end, 330 settlers—more than a quarter of the colony's population—were dead.

Because Opechancanough assumed that such a successful assault would drive the English out of Powhatan territory and back to England where they belonged, he did not mount another raid until September. Instead of fleeing, however, the English became determined to destroy the Powhatan tribes.

The English cut down the Indians' crops, smashed their canoes and temples, burned entire villages, and killed any stray Indians they came across. In May 1623, seeking a truce so that both sides could plant crops, Opechancanough met with English leaders. At the end of the peace talks, toasts were made. But the English had poisoned the Indians' drinks. As some Indians became ill and collapsed to the ground and others

continued on page 57

PAMUNKEY POTTERY

For more than 200 years, the Pamunkey Indians have made pottery, pipes, and other objects out of clay. These potters, most of them women, traditionally made dishes, pots, and jars for their own use and also sold some to non-Indians.

After they dug up the clay, potters mixed it with ground-up shells to strengthen it. They then shaped it by hand and rubbed it smooth with a shell or stone. Sometimes they scratched patterns into the pots before placing them in a fire to harden.

Over the years, these handmade objects were slowly replaced by manufactured kitchenware. In the 1930s, however, the Pamunkeys revived the art and began selling pottery to tourists. A pottery school was set up on the Pamunkey reservation by the state of Virginia. There the Pamunkeys could practice their craft and learn non-Indian methods of pottery making. Today, some Pamunkey artists make clay pots on potter's wheels, paint them with glaze, and fire them in kilns. Others, however, still work in the traditional style, keeping alive the ways of their ancestors.

A clay pipe bowl, about 4¼ inches high. This object and those on the next two pages were acquired in 1892–93 from Pamunkey chief Terrill Bradby by ethnologist J. G. Pollard.

A handcrafted cup with 3 legs, measuring 5 inches high and 2½ inches in diameter.

A pipe bowl, about two inches high. The multiple stems allowed five people to smoke it at once.

A two-inch-high pipe bowl. The Pamunkey may have learned to make multistemmed pipe bowls from their Catawba Indian neighbors.

A painted oval jar, 5¼ inches high. This and the other objects on these two pages were probably made by students at the Pamunkey pottery school in the 1930s and 1940s.

This Pamunkey jar, painted with a delicate swirling pattern, measures only 3¾ inches high.

A jar, 4½ inches high. The Pamunkey used cords, reeds, pointed sticks, or their fingernails to carve designs into wet clay.

A crosshatch design has been etched into this 3¾-inch jar.

A heavily glazed bowl, about 4½ inches in diameter and painted with white, green, purple, and black pigments. This object and the other two shown here were probably made in the mid-20th century. All are characteristic of the pottery school tradition.

A bowl, 4½ inches in diameter. The designs may have been inspired by those on southwestern tribes' pottery.

A painted 3½-inch vase. Teachers at the pottery school introduced the Pamunkey to pan-Indian designs—patterns used not only by their tribe but by Indians across the country.

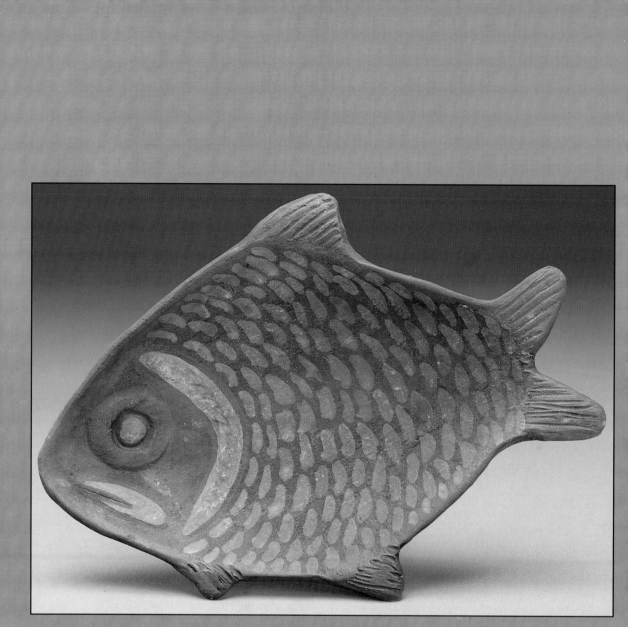

A fish-shaped dish, eight inches long and six inches wide, made in the
1930s. Aquatic motifs were popular with Pamunkey potters throughout the
20th century.

continued from page 48

attempted to escape, the English opened fire on them. Although Opechancanough was poisoned, he survived.

War dragged on for another 10 years. Although a decade of peace followed that, it brought little relief to the Powhatans. As disease decimated the Indians' population, the English settlements expanded. By 1640, there were about 8,100 British colonists in Virginia; the Native American population had fallen below 5,000.

The colonists had an insatiable hunger for land on which to grow tobacco. Because tobacco produced quick wealth, they always wanted more and more land. Growing tobacco also used up the nutrients in the soil very quickly, so the same land could not be farmed for very many years in a row. The constant need for wnew farmland led to steady encroachment on the Indians' territory.

On April 18, 1644, Opechancanough made one last attempt to oust the colonists from his territory. His warriors killed 400 settlers in the opening attack, but the British presence was now so large that they easily regrouped and went on the offensive. After two years of devastating English raids, the Powhatans could resist no longer.

In 1646, Opechancanough was captured and taken to Jamestown. Although he was over 80 years old and unable to walk without help, he never acknowledged defeat. He refused to sign a treaty. After being in prison only a short time, he was shot in the back by an English guard.

Necotowance, his successor, did sign a treaty. This treaty conceded that Necotowance was a subject of the king of England. As evidence of the king's rule over his territory, Necotowance agreed to pay a tribute of 20 beaver skins every year to the colonial governor. The treaty gave the English possession of the lowlands between the James and York rivers. The only Powhatans permitted to enter this territory were messengers from Necotowance, and they had to wear striped shirts. Any other Native American who entered this region would be shot on sight.

Necotowance lost power after 1649. From then on, each Powhatan tribe was ruled by its individual werowance. The empire that Powhatan had built had vanished.

To protect their territory from further English expansion, three werowances asked the colonial legislature for grants of land for their tribes. The legislature agreed to allow the tribes to keep for themselves certain pieces of land, known as reservations. But the settlers were greedy for the Indians' fertile lands. Ignoring the boundaries set by law, they moved onto the reservations. Although the Indians complained to the colonial government, they were forced onto smaller and smaller pieces of land.

None of the reservations were large enough to sustain the Powhatans' traditional way of life. The land, though adequate for farming, was not sufficient for hunting and gathering. Under these circumstances, many Indians were forced to work for the English in order to survive.

A few Indians worked in the colony itself as servants. Many of these servants had been captured by the English during wars and had never been released. Their status was very similar to that of the African slaves. Colonists had begun buying slaves in 1619, and their numbers were increasing rapidly.

Indian children were sometimes sent by their parents to work for white families. Although the children were supposed to be released from servitude when they turned 25, they were often not allowed to leave. In many cases, colonists simply kidnapped children, and if questioned, they claimed that the child's parents or werowance had sold the child to them.

Some Powhatan women earned money by selling traditional goods such as baskets, pipes, and pottery, but they had to change the design of these items to suit English tastes. For instance, they made pots with handles and legs to be used for cooking in fireplaces, as was the British custom.

Some Powhatan men were hired as hunters. Because wolves threatened British livestock, the colonists offered the Indians money to kill the animals. But the Powhatans believed that the reason to hunt was to acquire food and skins, not simply to kill. Since they did not eat wolf meat, very few Indians earned money by killing wolves. Other Powhatans worked as guides or built weirs for the English.

Many interactions between the Powhatans and colonists were more strained. Problems frequently arose because settlers let their hogs, which were identified only by a mark on their ear, roam freely through the woods. The Powhatans were used to hunting whatever game they found in the forests, so they sometimes killed Englishmen's hogs. Once, after apologizing to a colonist whose hogs were killed, a werowance also pointed out that the English had killed some of his deer. The colonist claimed there was a difference because the pigs were marked and the deer were not. The werowance replied, "Indeed, none of my deer are marked, and by that you may know them to be mine; and when you meet with any that are marked you may do with them what you please; for they are none of mine."

The 1670s saw great economic unrest among the settlers. High taxes, low tobacco prices, and drought made life difficult for them. Although the colonists were actually angry with their own political leadership, they took out their frustrations on the Indians. After being wrongly attacked and imprisoned, a group of Indians broke out of the fort where they were held. They later raided some plantations in revenge. Using this incident as an excuse, a group of rebellious Englishmen under the leadership of Nathaniel Bacon made war against the Powhatans. This was the last major military confrontation between colonists and Indians in the Tidewater. Bacon's men forced the Pamunkeys out of their village and hunted them down in a nearby swamp. Many of the Indians were killed, and the others were captured and paraded through the streets of Jamestown.

In May 1677, a new treaty was signed that reaffirmed the Powhatans' status as subjects of the British crown. It also established new, smaller reservations for the tribes. But again the settlers paid no attention to the boundaries.

Although contact with the colonists had altered aspects of the Powhatans' traditional

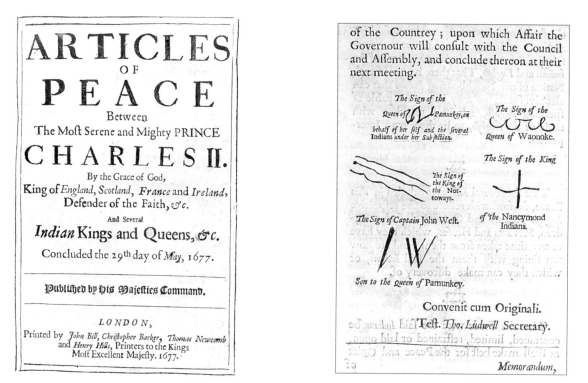

The title and signature pages of a 1677 treaty between several Tidewater tribes and the king of England.

culture, in 1700 that culture was still strong. Most Powhatan men continued to hunt, although they used guns instead of bows and arrows. With guns, they did not need to worry about getting their hair tangled, so they wore it long on both sides. Although their clothing styles remained the same, the clothes were often made from cloth rather than skins. Most Powhatans continued to follow their traditional religion. They still spoke their native language, but most could also speak some English. Despite being surrounded by whites—by this time in Virginia there were 100,000 colonists and less than 1,000 Indians—the Powhatans fought tenaciously to maintain their culture.

While the number of Indians was dropping, the number of black slaves in the region was booming. To Virginia's whites, race was all-important. A person was defined as either white or nonwhite, and all nonwhites were considered inferior. In 1705, the colony passed a "black code," a series of laws concerning race. Although Indians who lived on reservations had special status, those who lived among whites were classified as nonwhites and were subject to the same restrictions as free blacks and mulattoes (people with mixed black and white ancestry). This meant that nonreservation Indians could not hold public office or serve as witnesses in court. Whites could not marry nonwhites, and any white woman who had a child by a nonwhite could be fined and made a servant. Any child with only one Indian parent—regardless of whether the other parent was black or white—was classified as a mulatto and not an Indian. Because of such laws, those Indians who had skin light enough to pass as white usually did so. Facing such discrimination, they had little reason to want to be considered Indians.

Indians on reservations fared little better than those living among whites. The Nansatico tribe complained to colonial authorities about whites settling on their territory. When the authorities did nothing, some Nansatico warriors took matters into their own hands by killing a white family. The colonial authorities arrested all 49 members of the tribe. Five men were found guilty and hanged. Despite being found not guilty, the rest were deported to the West Indies. With a single stroke, an entire tribe was wiped out.

Meanwhile, other reservations shrank, and Indian populations dwindled. Tribes merged or *disintegrated*. Some Indians *assimilated* into white society; others joined free black communities. By the end of the 18th century, only the Pamunkeys and the Accomacs still had reservations and were officially recognized as Indians.

As a result, much of Powhatan culture was lost. By 1800, most Powhatans had become Christians. Their language was virtually extinct, a situation noted in 1787 by future U.S. president Thomas Jefferson in his book *Notes on the State of Virginia*. He wrote, "The Pamunkies are reduced to about 10 or 12 men. . . . The older ones among them preserve their language in a small degree, which are the last vestiges on earth, as far as we know, of the Powhatan language."

Although the Powhatan language disappeared, some of its words remain in use. Many cities and rivers in Virginia still bear Powhatan names. *Moccasin, tomahawk, raccoon,* and *opossum* are all words that the Powhatan language contributed to English.

During the early 19th century, southern whites' racial attitudes hardened. As they became more worried about the work of northern abolitionists—people who wanted to end the institution of slavery—and the possibility of slave revolts, they enacted stricter laws governing the activities of free nonwhites. Nonwhites had to carry certificates proving that they were free. Without these certificates, they could be jailed. If no one testified to their freedom, they could be sold into slavery. It became illegal for nonwhites to lead meetings and have guns. They also lost the right to jury trials; instead, justices decided their fates, just as they did with slaves.

Such laws made it necessary for Powhatans to be able to prove their "Indianness." Although reservation Indians remained exempt from some of these laws, their status was constantly threatened. As the Civil War approached, only the Pamunkeys still had official recognition. To survive, they would have to struggle to maintain their identity as Indians. ◭

A 1918 photograph of George Major Cook, chief of the Pamunkey Indians. By the end of the 19th century, many Indian men wore their hair long to proclaim their Indian identity.

Chapter **6**

Struggle for Survival

The conclusion of the Civil War in 1865 put an end to slavery in the United States. All blacks in the South were freed. In Virginia, the war's end also brought new definitions of "colored person" and "Indian." An 1866 law stated, "Every person having one-fourth or more of negro blood shall be deemed a colored person, and every person not a colored person having one-fourth or more of Indian blood shall be deemed an Indian." Thus, to be legally considered an Indian, a person had to be at least one-fourth Native American but less than one-fourth black.

67

After the war's end, whites retained their dominance in southern society. Most whites still believed they were naturally superior to blacks. Laws were passed keeping the races separated in public spaces, a concept called segregation. Blacks were not allowed to ride in train cars, attend schools, eat in restaurants, use bathrooms or water fountains, or live in houses that were reserved for whites. The facilities for blacks were far inferior to those for whites.

Because of such laws, the Powhatans fought hard to keep their Indian status. If they were considered colored instead of Indian, they would be treated as badly as blacks. For instance, only reservation Indians could ride in the railroad cars reserved for whites. Those who lived off reservations suffered the indignity of riding in the "colored" car. So the Powhatans began forming their own institutions to proclaim their Indian identity. In 1865, they established their own church, the Pamunkey Indian Baptist Church.

They demanded separate schools from blacks for their children, who were not allowed in white schools. This antagonized whites who did not want to pay for another set of schools. But it also angered blacks. They thought that, since they were both oppressed by whites, the Indians should be their allies rather than try to separate themselves.

The schools for Native Americans offered limited curriculums. The only one that taught anything about Native American culture was a pottery school established on the Pamunkey reservation in 1932. But even there, a white teacher taught the students to use a pottery wheel instead of teaching them to make pottery in the traditional way. The teacher also showed the students how to make designs he thought were typically "Indian" but which actually had nothing to do with their culture.

Because of the discrimination they suffered if they were considered colored, many Powhatans tried to make themselves more easily identifiable as Indians. This was not easy because their traditional way of life was almost completely gone, and they were now living like white people. Even the Pamunkeys had to constantly prove that they were really Indians. They sometimes dressed in Indian fashion at public events. But the way the Powhatans had traditionally dressed—wearing virtually nothing—would not have been acceptable in 19th-century Virginia. So instead they wore outfits based on the clothing of other tribes—large headdresses and suede pants, shirts, and dresses that were decorated with fringes and beads.

Because there were so few Indians in Virginia, the Powhatans tried to find other Native Americans to marry. According to the racial purity laws, if they married non-Indians their children would not legally be considered Indian. To find spouses, the Pamunkeys advertised in newspapers from North Carolina to Oklahoma. But Virginia was known as a harsh place for nonwhites, so they had little success.

Although the Pamunkeys had long been the only tribe recognized by Virginia, the Powhatans' pride and the value of legal

Chickahominy leaders pay their tribe's annual tribute to the governor of Virginia in 1919.

Indian status led other tribes to organize. The Pamunkey reservation had been divided into two pieces in the 18th century. In 1894, those living in the part along the Mattaponi River split into a separate tribe called the Mattaponis. In 1901, Indians living off reservations organized a tribe called the Chickahominys. Another group, the Eastern Chickahominys, split off in 1925. Two other tribes, the Upper Mattaponis and the Rappahannocks, organized in the 1920s. But even then, only the Pamunkeys and the Mattaponis had reservations and were recognized by the state.

As the Powhatan tribes organized, Virginia made its racial definitions stricter. In 1924, Virginia turned the "one-drop rule" into law. This rule stated that no one could be called white who had one drop of blood from any other race. The only exceptions were people who were less than $\frac{1}{16}$ Native American: they could still be considered white. This loophole was made for the benefit of the many ruling class whites in Virginia who claimed to be descended from Pocahontas and John Rolfe. The one-drop rule would have forced them to be considered colored, so an exception was made for their sake.

The new law said that nonreservation Indians had to be at least $\frac{1}{4}$ Native American and could not have one drop of black blood. Indians on reservations were still considered Indians only if they were less than $\frac{1}{16}$ black.

Walter Plecker, the head of Virginia's Bureau of Vital Statistics, cruelly enforced this law. He forced the Powhatans to prove they had no black ancestry. But Indian birth certificates and other records, particularly for those living off reservations, were not kept systematically, and many of Virginia's records had been destroyed during the Civil War. Proving Indian heritage was virtually impossible.

Plecker threatened all Powhatans by trying to prove that none of them were Indians. He studied records dating back to 1830. Although the word "colored" was not used in the same way at that time, he assumed it was. If the word was used in an old document, he designated the persons' descendants as colored. He also tried to force county clerks to identify newborn Indian babies as colored. Some bowed to his pressure; others did not. In 1924, he went so far as to say that there were no Indians in Virginia who did not have some black ancestry. To him, this meant that there were no Indians in Virginia.

Plecker's harassment had far-reaching consequences for the Powhatans. Indian children were ejected from white schools,

In the 20th century, several Tidewater tribes have won official recognition from the state of Virginia.

and Plecker threatened a Chickahominy midwife with criminal prosecution, claiming she had falsified records when she wrote "Indian" on a birth certificate. The pressure against the Powhatans was so intense that some moved to northeastern states, where there was less discrimination and people were unlikely to question their heritage. The Powhatans struggled against Plecker's policies until 1946, when he finally retired.

Beginning in the 1950s, the civil rights movement slowly eroded segregation in America. Indians as well as blacks benefited from the civil rights movement. It enabled Powhatans to hold government positions in Virginia for the first time. In the 1970s in Charles City County, a Chickahominy was hired as a county administrator; two Indians held positions on the county planning commission; and another Chickahominy served on the county school board. Other Powhatans have become teachers, doctors, lawyers, and accountants.

A funeral procession by members of the Mattaponi tribe honoring Chief Jacob Vincent Custalow, also known as Thundercloud, in 1982.

The Indian rights movement, which began in the 1960s, increased the Powhatans' visibility and pride. All across the United States, Native Americans joined together to fight for their rights. The movement helped the Pamunkeys mount a lawsuit against the Southern Railway Company. In 1855, the railroad took 22 acres of the Pamunkey reservation to lay a track. The company paid the tribe nothing for the land. In 1971, the Pamunkeys accepted an out-of-court settlement of $100,000, future rent on the land, and the return of seven acres that were not being used by the railroad.

In the past two decades, the Powhatan tribes have thrived. In addition to the Pamunkeys and the Mattaponis, Virginia now also formally recognizes the Eastern and Western Chickahominys, the Upper Mattaponis, the Rappahannocks, and the Nansemonds. This represents great progress compared to 100 years ago, when the state recognized only the Pamunkeys.

Nearly 400 years after the arrival of British colonists in North America, the descendants of the Powhatans have endured. They have outlived early efforts to slaughter them and later efforts to claim they simply did not exist. Above all, they have never forgotten who they are and have remained proud and visible as Native Americans. ▲

GLOSSARY

abduct kidnap

assimilate become a member of a different group of people and adopt their way of life

charisma the ability of a leader to inspire love and loyalty in others

colonial having to do with a settlement or colony ruled by a distant country

crescent a narrow, curved moon shape

disintegrate break apart

epidemic a serious outbreak of disease that strikes a large group of people

immunity the body's natural ability to fight off disease

loincloth a simple garment hanging from the waist

mission a settlement of people attempting to spread their religion in a foreign land

missionary a person who travels to a foreign land to convert the native population to Christianity

puberty the age at which a child's body changes to that of an adult

sapling a small tree

scaffold an open framework

sinew tough fibers that connect muscles to other parts of the body

stratified divided into separate classes

tan make leather from animal skins by treating them with tree bark or materials rich in tannin

tribute gifts or payments to a ruler

vengeful intent on inflicting punishment or revenge

CHRONOLOGY

1520s   First contact between Europeans and Native Americans in the Chesapeake Bay region occurs

1560   Spanish establish colony in the area

late 16th century   Powhatan inherits power over eight tribes and brings another 20 tribes under his control

1607   British colonists found Jamestown, the first permanent English settlement in North America

ca. 1608   Pocahontas allegedly saves Captain John Smith, one of the settlement's leaders

1613   Samuel Argall kidnaps Pocahontas, and she is converted to Christianity

1614   Pocahontas marries John Rolfe

1622   Opechancanough leads an attack on English settlers; 330 are killed

1677   Treaty is signed that reaffirms the Powhatans' status as subjects of the British crown

1705   The colony passes a "black code," a series of racial laws

1790   The Pamunkeys and Accomacs are the only tribes that have reservations and are recognized as Indians

1855   The Southern Railway Company takes 22 acres of the Pamunkey reservation to lay a track

1865   Indians establish their own church, the Pamunkey Indian Baptist Church

1971   The Pamunkeys accept an out-of-court settlement from the Southern Railway Company for $100,000, the return of seven acres, and future rent on the remaining land.

INDEX

A

Accomac Indians, 64
Appamatuck, 36
Argall, Samuel, 42

B

Bacon, Nathaniel, 61
Black code, 63
Bureau of Vital Statistics,
    Virginia, 72

C

Canoes, 17, 19, 48
Charles City County, Virginia, 74
Chesapeake Bay, 8, 13, 35, 36
Chickahominy Indians, 71, 73, 74
Christianity, 35, 36, 42, 47, 64
Civil rights movement, 74
Civil War, the, 65, 67, 72
"Colored persons," 67
Copper, 24, 25, 26, 27, 28, 40
Councillors, 23, 26, 33

D

Don Luis, 35–36

E

Eastern Chickahominy Indians,
    71, 75
England, 38, 42, 48, 58
English, 8, 10–11, 13, 24, 36, 37,
    38, 40, 41, 42, 46, 47, 48, 57,
    59, 60, 62, 75
Europe, 46

F

Free blacks, 64

H

Huskenaw, 29–30

I

Indians rights movement, 75
Influenza, 45

J

James River, 8, 36, 58
Jamestown, Virginia, 8, 10,
    36–37, 38, 41–43, 57, 61
Jefferson, Thomas, 64

M

Mamanatowick, 33, 45
Maryland, 8
Matrilineal succession, 23
Mattaponi Indians, 71, 75
Mattaponi River, 71
Measles, 45
Missionaries, 36, 47
Mulattoes, 63

N

Nansatico Indians, 63–64
Nansemond Indians, 75
Necotowance (Powhatan chief),
    58
North America, 8, 11, 75
North Carolina, 70
Notes on the State of Virginia
    (Jefferson), 64

O

Okewas (Powhatan god), 25, 26,
    30
Oklahoma, 70
"One-drop rule," 71
Opechancanough (Powhatan
    chief), 40, 45, 47–58
Opichapam (Powhatan chief), 45

P

Pamunkey Indian Baptist Church,
    68
Pamunkey Indian Reservation,
    69, 71, 75
Pamunkey Indians, 61, 64, 65,
    69, 70, 71, 75
Paspahegh, 41
Plecker, Walter, 72–74

Pocahontas, 9–10, 40, 42, 71
Portuguese, 35
Potomac Indians, 8
Powhatan, 8, 9, 10, 33, 37, 38,
    40, 41, 42, 43, 45, 58
Powhatan Indians
  children, 15, 20, 21, 26, 28, 29–
      30, 33, 41, 46, 59, 72, 73
  and Christianity, 36, 42, 64, 68
  clothing, 19–20, 62, 69–70
  crafts, 15, 26–28, 59–60, 69
  creation myth, 7–8
  and disease, 25, 45–46, 57
  education, 68, 69, 72
  Europeans, contact with, 8–11,
      33, 35–65, 69
  farming, 15, 16, 21, 40, 45, 59
  fishing, 17–18
  games, 20–21
  hunting, 16, 18–19, 21, 26, 59,
      60, 62
  jewelry, 26–28
  language, 62, 64–65
  marriage, 30–31, 33, 70
  and racism, 63, 65, 67–74
  religion, 7–8, 15, 25–26, 32–33,
      62, 64, 68
  and reservations, 58, 61, 63,
      64, 65, 68, 69
  trade, 38, 40, 41
  treaties, 58, 61
  tribal politics, 15, 23–25, 26, 33
  warfare, 19, 26, 36, 37, 41, 48–
      58, 61
  women, 15–17,19, 23–24, 26,
      27, 28, 29, 30, 41, 59
Priests, 25–26, 29, 33

R
Racial purity laws, 67, 70, 71
Rappahannock Indians, 71, 75

Rolfe, John, 42, 46, 71
Rolfe, Thomas, 42
Ruling families, 23

S
Segregation, 68, 74
Slavery, 59, 63, 65, 67
Smallpox, 45
Smith, John, 9–10, 28, 39–40
Southern Railway Company, 75
Spanish, 35

T
Tattoos, 28
Temples, 25–26, 32, 41, 48
Tidewater region, 13, 18, 33
Tobacco, 15, 25, 46, 47, 57, 61

U
United States, 10, 74
Upper Mattaponi Indians, 71, 75

V
Virginia, 8, 11, 13, 42, 46, 47, 57,
    62, 63, 65, 67, 69, 70, 71, 72,
    74, 75

W
Weronsquas, 23–24
Werowances, 23–25, 26, 32, 33,
    58, 59, 60
Werowocomoco, 40
Western Chickahominy Indians,
    75
West Indies, 64

Y
York River, 58

ABOUT THE AUTHOR

MELISSA MCDANIEL is a freelance writer and editor living in New York City. Her other books for children include *The Sac and Fox Indians* and a young adult biography of Stephen Hawking.

PICTURE CREDITS

Daily Press, Inc., Newport News, VA: p. 74; The Denver Art Museum: pp. 52, 53, 56; Department of Anthropology, Smithsonian Institution: pp. 49, 50, 51, 54, 55; Jamestown-Yorktown Foundation: p. 14; Library of Congress: pp. 2, 8, 12, 17, 22, 27, 32, 34, 39, 45, 46; National Museum of the American Indian, Smithsonian Institution: p. 66; National Park Service, Colonial National Historic Park: p. 38; New York Public Library, Astor, Lenox, and Tilden Foundations: p. 62; Smithsonian Institution: p. 70.

Maps by Gary Tong: pp. 6, 73.